Second Edition

WRITE
to be
READ

Reading, Reflection, and Writing

TEACHER'S MANUAL

WILLIAM R. SMALZER

CAMBRIDGE
UNIVERSITY PRESS

CAMBRIDGE UNIVERSITY PRESS
Cambridge, New York, Melbourne, Madrid, Cape Town, Singapore, São Paulo

Cambridge University Press
40 West 20th Street, New York, NY 10011-4211, USA

www.cambridge.org
Information on this title: www.cambridge.org/9780521547475

First published 2005
2nd printing 2005

Printed in the United States of America

ISBN-13   978-0-521-54747-5
ISBN-10   0-521-54747-4

CONTENTS

PREFACE

Write to Be Read: Reading, Reflection, and Writing is a high intermediate to advanced writing text designed to teach English language learners to write convincing paragraphs and academic essays with greater fluency. The second edition includes seven new readings and one entirely new chapter, "Questions of Right and Wrong." In addition, more attention is given to reading preparation and vocabulary development. For the first of the two readings in each chapter, there is a vocabulary exercise that introduces challenging vocabulary and also serves as a preview of the reading. For the second reading, which is generally shorter, important vocabulary is introduced in background notes and in the reflection and discussion activity.

Influenced by the whole language approach, *Write to Be Read* focuses primarily on discovering and communicating meaning rather than on learning discrete skills. The methodology is a blend of both the process and product approaches to writing. The process approach encourages students to develop their thinking about a topic through reading, writing, discussion, and revision. The product approach, relying heavily on student essays as models, helps writing students meet the expectations of their audience, educated readers of English.

Though much of writing is a solitary activity, *Write to Be Read* makes ample use of collaborative activities in discussions of readings and topics, in prewriting activities, and in peer review. The educational design of the book encourages students to think more clearly and critically and to develop their own voices as writers. The text also stresses the importance of summarizing and paraphrasing when using others' writing.

Readings include selections from nonfiction books, short stories, fables, essays, speeches, and magazine articles. Writing instruction concentrates on the academic essay, which is seen as the basis for other forms of academic writing. Of the seven chapters, the first two are devoted to paragraphs and the next five to essays. Chapters 6 and 7 discuss persuasive and argument essays. Appendix A has additional exercises on sentence structure, grammar, and punctuation for students who need such work. Appendix B, in the Student Book only, gives complete essay assessment guidelines.

After becoming familiar with the topic of each chapter through reflection, discussion, and reading, students prepare for the formal writing assignment in stages. In each chapter, they begin with expressive writing and progress to more objective academic writing. First, in private journals, students respond subjectively to the main reading. Then they write responses that are more objective and share them with an audience of peers in Part 2. In Part 3, students read a second selection and think critically about the topic. After turning their attention to writing skills in Part 4, students begin the formal writing assignment in Part 5. They prepare a first draft after completing exercises designed to generate ideas and expand their points of view. Then they revise their first drafts, get feedback from peers, and revise further before submitting essays for the teacher's evaluation.

Progressing from private, subjective writing to public, objective writing in each chapter helps students develop their thinking about topics one step at a time. It also develops a sense of audience and purpose in writing. The thinking/writing process is enhanced by collaborative work in which comprehension of meaning (the reader's goal) and expression of meaning (the writer's goal) guide most tasks.

William R. Smalzer

INTRODUCTION

Every chapter of *Write to Be Read* contains five parts:

1 INTRODUCTION TO THE TOPIC, READING, AND DISCUSSION

2 PERSONAL WRITTEN RESPONSE

3 FURTHER READING, WRITING, AND DISCUSSION

4 FOCUS ON WRITING SKILLS

5 FORMAL WRITING ASSIGNMENT

What follows is information for the teacher about the organization of each of these parts and suggestions for how to use them.

1   INTRODUCTION TO THE TOPIC, READING, AND DISCUSSION ···········

The first part of every chapter includes activities designed to develop schema and prepare students for the first reading selection. Through reflection on the topic, discussion, a vocabulary exercise, and notes on the first reading, students prepare to read. Comprehension questions lead students to read for the overall meaning first and then to delve more deeply as well as bring their own experience to the text.

Teachers who prefer that students do some writing from the start could assign them to write answers to questions in sections B and E, *Discussion* and *Reading for More Detail,* respectively. However, students who write out their answers will still benefit from sharing and comparing their answers orally, and will then be better prepared for the oral and written aspects of the rest of the chapter.

Some students will automatically read the selection more than once, while others will want only one reading. As a general principle, if students are not satisfied with their comprehension after the two readings called for in the directions, they should read the text a third time, noting areas where they still have trouble and will need help during class discussion of the reading. In the end, how many times a student reads a selection will be the student's decision since it is recommended that reading be done as homework.

2 PERSONAL WRITTEN RESPONSE ·····································

The second part of every chapter is an important component of the process approach of *Write to Be Read*. Students will think, read, and write better if they respond *subjectively* to the main reading at this point. Furthermore, it is recommended that the teacher not collect writing from this part of the chapter. By not collecting this writing, the teacher will help students understand the concept of audience. What students have to say to themselves and to classmates is likely different from what they might write for a teacher. Students are asked to choose two topics and write for 20 minutes. If they have a lot to say about one topic, they can certainly devote the whole time to that single topic.

To keep students accountable for this writing, teachers may want to devise a record-keeping system. Teachers whose students do the assignments on a word processor at the school's facility might find a way to check students' directories without actually reading their writing. Teachers who are tempted to collect and read this writing run the risk of distorting students' perception of who the real audience is.

For section C, *Feedback on Your Writing,* to be developmental, it should be nonthreatening. That is why listeners are instructed to listen, to take notes, to summarize, and to question but not to criticize. Having students listen to each other's writing rather than read it keeps them from focusing on mechanical errors. At this point, they have more important things to attend to, namely content and organization. The oral format is also a change from an emphasis on reading and writing in Part 1 and the preceding sections of Part 2 and is an authentic communication activity. It allows aural learners a chance to shine and quieter ones a chance to practice speaking after some thought and preparation.

The *Peer Feedback Guidelines* on page 11 of the Student Book outline a procedure for sharing and responding to each other's writing. The guidelines should be reviewed with the class from the start and discussed as a nonthreatening tool for developing the students' own writing as well as their sensitivity to others' writing.

3 FURTHER READING, WRITING, AND DISCUSSION ·····················

Part 3 contains the second reading selection on the chapter topic, which is from a different genre and features a different perspective. By the time students reach this part, they already have a good grasp of the topic and a knowledge of relevant vocabulary. The aim is to take students further into the topic while encouraging them to read–and think–more independently. Students are still helped with new vocabulary but less than in Part 1. Instead, students are asked to negotiate the meaning among themselves through writing and, later, through discussion. For students who have not demonstrated reasonable comprehension of the reading during peer feedback, a teacher may want to ask volunteers to share their responses with the whole class. Or the teacher may have students identify passages that they found difficult. In general, these second reading selections have been kept shorter and somewhat easier than the main readings to facilitate students' negotiation of the meaning on their own.

Write to Be Read does not aim so much to give students something to say as to help them think and discover their own points of view on topics. In particular, section E, *Discussion: Critical Thinking,* may be challenging for students who are used to scanning for factual answers or answers that can be lifted directly from the text. The questions in this section are designed to make students think about the topics, thereby promoting critical thinking skills such as comparison, inference, and evaluation.

Additionally, classes that do not have an academic emphasis could use the critical thinking questions as writing topics in place of the more academic topics suggested for the formal writing assignment in Part 5. Teachers who wish to de-emphasize the academic may also choose to omit Part 4, section B, *Meeting Reader Expectations,* as well as Part 5, section A, *Writing Topics.*

4 FOCUS ON WRITING SKILLS ···

Using Another's Writing, the first section in Part 4, asks students to paraphrase or summarize others' writing. Both are difficult skills but important ones, especially for students who come from a tradition of using professional writing to bolster their own. What may be a normal use of another's writing in some cultures can be plagiarism in academic contexts in others.

Skilled writers often use another's writing directly, with documentation, when it expresses an idea better than they themselves can express it. For language learners, however, this condition applies to nearly all of their writing. Moreover, there are substantial language benefits that accrue from thinking about the meaning of passages and expressing that meaning in one's own words. Therefore, students should learn early on that copying is unacceptable and that they need to learn to paraphrase and summarize instead.

An essential first step in paraphrasing and summarizing is understanding the material well. This requires that students read and reread each passage carefully. Writing the paraphrase will be difficult for students initially; the key lies in either changing the structure of the original sentence or in beginning with another grammatical subject. It might be useful to practice paraphrasing some examples with students. For example, one could begin with this sentence (lines 29–30) from "How Your Birth Order Influences Your Life Adjustment" on page 6 of Chapter 1:

"The parents themselves have been <u>changed</u> by the <u>preceding</u> child or children in many ways."

Teach the students to paraphrase this sentence by following these steps:

1 Write the sentence on the board with two words underlined as shown. After students have found the sentence in the reading and understood it in its context, write *The children . . .* as the first words of the paraphrase on the board.

2 Elicit suggestions for ways to continue. Allow each student to contribute a maximum of three words without using any of the words underlined in the original sentence.

3 Write whatever a student offers, and let other students judge its correctness and appropriateness.

4 Erase errors that students identify; silently point to errors they overlook.

5 Continue building the paraphrase word by word, phrase by phrase. You might end up with the following:

> *The children   who came before   have made   the parents different people   than they were   in many ways.*

6 Highlight a phrase or two at a time to see if a better paraphrase might result from revision. The paraphrase in step 5, with some more thought and attention to the original, could become:

> *Previous children have caused the parents themselves to become different people in several respects.*

7 Ask students which of the two versions of the paraphrase they prefer and why.

In section B in Part 4, *Meeting Reader Expectations,* students learn standard English rhetoric: form, organization, and logic. Authentic student essays (and one teacher essay) illustrate the points of rhetoric discussed and support the product approach of *Write to Be Read.* Teachers may wish to use the models to illustrate the *Essay Assessment Checklist* found at the end of each chapter, beginning with Chapter 3. Using the assessment checklist in this way will get students ready to assess their own writing and familiarize them with their teacher's expectations. However, teachers may have their own guidelines for paragraphs and essays, which, of course, can be used in place of the ones provided.

The next section in Part 4 targets sentence structure. It is often the case that students make more rather than fewer errors in sentence structure as they progress in writing, and this is understandable if disconcerting. As they progress, students attempt longer and more sophisticated sentences, which are more prone to errors in sentence structure. Section C in Part 4, *Sentence Grammar*, provides the help most students at this level need to keep their meaning from being obscured by poor sentence structure.

While teachers are rightly concerned about more common word-level errors students make in their writing, the author has found it more effective to do this work separate from the students' compositions. Errors in verb, noun, and adjective forms as well as in other areas of grammar certainly need attention, especially if they obscure meaning. If students make a lot of errors and teachers stress error correction, students will unconsciously shift their focus from *writing* to *grammar*. Normally, students at this level have received much more instruction in grammar than in writing; teachers should make an effort to keep the focus on writing. There are hints for individualizing grammar work while separating it from the writing piece in *Suggestions for Teaching and Assessment* later in this Introduction.

Classes or individual students that require more focus on word order, adjectives and adverbs, relative clauses, punctuation, or additional work in sentence structure will benefit from the exercises in Appendix A of the Student Book.

5   FORMAL WRITING ASSIGNMENT ···

Section A of Part 5, *Writing Topics,* offers students a choice of essay topics related to the chapter readings. However, since students put more work into topics that appeal to them, they should suggest their own topics if none of the ones provided inspires them. If a student discovers midway through the writing process that he or she has nothing to say or no interest in the topic, there are two solutions: switching to another topic or putting more thought into the original topic. "I don't have anything to say" often means the student has not thought deeply or carefully about the topic. Other times, the teacher's suggestion of a slight modification in the topic will get the student back on track.

Section B, *Generating Ideas,* sometimes meets with opposition from students, who may not yet have made the connection between more thinking and better writing. Experienced writers realize how freewriting, looping, mind mapping, discussion, and debating lead to clearer thinking, and, therefore, better writing. Less experienced writers may see activities such as free writing as tedious or as a waste of time. Students may need to be encouraged and even pushed a bit until they see the benefit of these invention strategies. Teachers may want to do prewriting activities in class until students develop the habit of prewriting on their own.

Section C, *Expanding Your Point of View,* aims to open students' minds to others' opinions through group discussions, interviews, and research. It is a logical extension of the previous section and a chance to refine and develop ideas.

If time permits, students could do some of the initial drafting of section D, *Initial Drafts,* in class. The teacher's help and comments are always welcomed by students. Rather than read what students have written so far, it is often better to have students explain out loud what they have written, summarize their main idea and support, and mention what problems they are having. This keeps the ownership of the writing in their hands and allows them to lead the conference. In the minute or two that a teacher might be able to devote to each student in informal in-class conferences, one cannot realistically read and consider every student's work carefully. And if a teacher reads an early draft and makes no specific criticism, the silence can be interpreted as tacit approval of what has been written. Teachers can keep the ball in the student's court by making sure that the student is doing most of the talking.

Like prewriting, revision can seem unnecessary to students who tend to think of their initial efforts as the last word on the subject. When revising, students need to look more closely at how thoroughly they have thought about the issues, how accurately their writing expresses what is actually in their minds, and how closely their draft matches the teacher's expectations of form, organization, and language use. Trying to keep all these considerations in mind while writing can be daunting. Writing the first draft more freely to get ideas down on paper helps to ease the process. Once their ideas are down on paper, writers can better evaluate their thinking, expression, form, organization, and language use in further drafts.

The writing topics lend themselves to academic paragraphs and essays. Students whose focus is not academic writing might skip *Meeting Reader Expectations* (Part 4, section B) but will probably benefit from exercises in Part 5 designed to help them generate ideas and expand their point of view. A nonacademic group might also skip the instructions in *Initial Drafts,* but will likely benefit from the assessment checklist (as provided in the Student Book or from the teacher) that deals with the writers' thinking, logic, audience, and voice.

As pointed out in *Suggestions for Teaching and Assessment,* below, the author prefers objective assessment to holistic grading. Each teacher must make his or her own choice, but the author recommends more objective assessment guidelines such as those in Appendix B of the Student Book. A number score based on objective assessment guidelines gives students more comprehensible feedback on how to revise a particular essay and improve their writing in general.

SUGGESTIONS FOR TEACHING AND ASSESSMENT

1 *Assign readings and drafts as homework.* To keep class lively, the readings in Parts 1 and 3 should be done by students on their own and discussed in class. Likewise, most drafts of paragraphs and essays can be written outside of class. However, students will benefit from occasionally writing in journals and doing the shared writing in Part 2 under time pressure in class because such exercises approximate exam situations.

2 *Use the photographs and illustrations to introduce topics.* Use the visuals at the beginning of Parts 1 and 3 as a warm-up, as a way to get students thinking about the topic, and as a means to elicit vocabulary related to the topic.

3 *Promote cooperation and collaboration.* Promote cooperation and collaboration among students by keeping the same small groups for *Feedback on Your Writing* (in Part 2), *Helping Each Other Understand* (in Part 3), *Expanding Your Point of View* (in Part 5), and *Peer Feedback* (also in Part 5) within the same chapter.

4 *Let students do their own writing.* Resist the temptation to take ownership of students' writing. Lead students to think, but do not think for them. If you wish, write the same assignments that your students do. Use your writing to illustrate revision, assessment, or other points. Sharing your writing with students takes courage but makes a valuable point: Even "good" writers need to revise.

5 *Have conferences with students.* Though schedules may not always allow, try to have a writing conference with each student, even for just two or three minutes, at some point during the drafting of each formal writing assignment. Students can learn to lead the conference by being ready to explain what stage they have reached in the writing process and what problems they are facing. The time is better spent if students ask you questions rather than vice versa. In a quick conference, it is better not to read a student's draft; there isn't enough time for you to judge the work fairly.

6 *Focus on writing, not grammar.* Help students realize that the course focuses more on clear writing than on correct grammar. Grammar does need to be dealt with, but it will keep the focus clearer if you refrain from marking every error. Instead, individualize grammar work by identifying for each student a few kinds of errors that occur in his or her work and assigning tasks that focus on these errors. For example, a set of tasks for a student might look like this:

Write new sentences with each of the following constructions:

1   even though / even if
2   look at / look for
3   because . . . / because of . . .
4   (adjective + er) than . . . / more (adjective) than . . .
5   . . . ; for example, . . .
6   went . . . ago / has gone . . . since

Students will need help understanding what to do with these instructions initially. They will soon catch on that you do not want them merely to rewrite sentences from their essays but to demonstrate an understanding of the grammar points by writing completely new sentences.

Teaching grammar outside the context of the students' compositions keeps the course focus on thinking and writing about ideas. Your specific and positive written comments on content, word choice, organization, and other points will assure students that you have read their papers carefully. Positive comments are also more motivating than lots of grammar corrections.

7 *Revise in class.* Help students understand the revision process by revising together in class. Use a former student's paper or your own.

8 *Limit the number of revisions.* Given the choice between reworking the same paper over and over and going on to a new topic, teachers and students will find it more productive to go on to a new topic. Students will benefit more from reading, thinking, and writing about a new topic than from spending too much time revising an old paper. Revision of writing is important, of course; consider using the portfolio approach to evaluation (see item 13) so that several weeks elapse before a final revision on a paper is due.

9 *Distinguish between assessment and grades.* Make a distinction between assessment, pointing out strengths and weaknesses, and evaluation, assigning a holistic letter grade. Once a letter grade is put on a paper, students will give the essay little further serious thought or work.

10 *Use analytical assessment.* Use analytical assessment, based on the guidelines provided, so that students understand what is expected and how a weak paper can be improved. A *Paragraph Assessment Checklist* is provided at the ends of Chapters 1 and 2, and an *Essay Assessment Checklist* is provided at the ends of Chapters 3–7. Elements in the checklist vary according to the focus of each chapter.

Appendix B includes more complete essay assessment guidelines with the characteristics of very good, average, and weak essays in all three areas of assessment: (1) content and ideas, (2) organization and form, and (3) language use. Revise or replace the guidelines if they do not fit your students or your way of teaching.

11 *Model how to assess a paper.* As a class, assess an outside paper or one of the student models in the book so that students will know how to use the guidelines when they revise their own essays. Alternatively, give your students examples of what you consider very good, average, and weak essays. Use papers from a previous class to avoid embarrassment.

12 *Give three separate scores.* In assessing a paper, give three separate scores, one each for content and ideas, organization and form, and language use so that students understand their strengths and weaknesses. For example, an analytical assessment of 8/10 (8 out of a possible score of 10) for content and ideas, 4/5 for organization and form, and 1/5 for language use indicates that the student has done well in two out of three areas. Weighting content and ideas twice as heavily as the other two categories lets students know that you feel that the logic, clarity, and sincerity of the thoughts expressed are the most important aspects of their papers.

13 *Use a portfolio approach.* If it works for your class, use a portfolio approach for evaluation. Rather than evaluate the formal writing assignments with a letter grade, assess them using the assessment guidelines and numerical scores. Then allow students to revise one of their already-assessed papers for a midterm grade and another paper for a final grade. The portfolio approach allows students to come back to their writing later with more insights into the topic, and with a better idea of rhetorical and language conventions because of intervening study. To avoid inflated grades, some teachers average the scores on successive revisions rather than considering only the last, best effort.

William R. Smalzer

PLANNING THE USE OF THE BOOK

Each of the seven chapters can be done in about two weeks in an intensive class meeting four or five hours a week. The author recommends that *Write to Be Read* be divided into class work and homework as below. Variations in routine are welcome in any class, however, and some variations on the plan below are set out in *General Organization and Guidelines* in the *Introduction*.

CLASS WORK

Part 1

A Reflection
B Discussion

Follow-ups to *Reading for Overall Meaning* and *Reading for More Detail*

Part 2

C Feedback on Your Writing

Part 3

A Preparing to read
    Reflection and Discussion
D Follow-up to *Helping Each Other Understand*
E Discussion: Critical Thinking

Part 5

B Generating Ideas
C Expanding Your Point of View
E Review, Revision, and Assessment
    Peer Feedback

HOMEWORK

Part 1

D Reading for Overall Meaning
E Reading for More Detail

Part 3

B Reading for Overall Meaning
C Reading for More Detail

Part 5

D Initial Drafts
E Review, Revision, and Assessment
   Further Revision

CLASS WORK OR HOMEWORK

Part 1

C Preparing to Read
   Notes on the Reading
   Previewing the Vocabulary

Part 2

A Journals: A Private Audience
B Shared Writing

Part 3

A Preparing to Read
   Notes on the Reading
D Helping Each Other Understand

Part 4

A Using Another's Writing
B Meeting Reader Expectations
C Sentence Grammar

Part 5

A Writing Topics

A NOTE REGARDING THIS TEACHER'S MANUAL

Following this introduction, the Teacher's Manual contains seven chapters and an appendix, Appendix A. Each of the seven chapters contains general comments about the corresponding chapter in the Student's Book, followed by an answer key to the exercises in that chapter. (Appendix A of the Teacher's Manual contains only an answer key.)

Not all of the exercises found in the Student's Book are covered in the Teacher's Manual. Only those exercises for which useful answers or comments could be provided have been included.

Birth Order and Your Place in Life

Chapter 1 concentrates on the paragraph. The main focus is on writing good topic sentences and supporting them adequately. Students who already have experience writing essays may choose to write an essay instead of a paragraph for their formal writing assignment. If they do, they may want to study the student model essay, "Different Stages of Friendship" on page 71 and the *Essay Assessment Checklist* at the end of Chapter 3.

However, when students progress from paragraphs to essays, there is sometimes a tendency for them to write weaker paragraphs because of the demands of the longer form. Since well-developed paragraphs are the foundation of a good essay, even students who are already writing essays may want to review the steps to effective paragraph writing in this chapter.

SPECIFIC COMMENTS AND ANSWER KEY

PART 1

INTRODUCTION TO THE TOPIC, READING, AND DISCUSSION

C Preparing to read

PREVIEWING THE VOCABULARY

Answers (page 3)

1 c	4 c	7 b	10 b	13 c
2 b	5 c	8 c	11 c	14 c
3 a	6 c	9 b	12 b	

D Reading for overall meaning

Answers (page 6)

Answers will vary according to each student's birth order. Students' answers to the question could be a good way to begin a discussion of the reading in class.

E Reading for more detail

Answers (page 8)

1 Oldest child:
   - initially, in a close, often intense relationship with parents that encourages imitation and learning
   - soon struggles to be parental
   - serves as a model to siblings; is a barrier between them and parents
   - is expected to be more capable and responsible
   - feels more adequate than siblings
   - expects others to be less capable

   Later children (both middle and youngest):
   - benefit from more relaxed parents in that there is less "experimenting"
   - do not feel as lonely or as inadequate
   - move gradually from child to adult

   Middle child:
   - sometimes feels better able to do things but is also able to ask for help
   - doesn't have clear expectations about abilities of others

   Youngest child:
   - feels less adequate but is not concerned as he/she can rely on others

   Only child:
   - sees others as more adequate but learns to be independent out of the realization that parents won't always be there

2 Individual answers will vary.

3 The answer is largely inferred. The oldest comes off seeming like the most responsible because he/she tries to be parental, serves as a model to younger siblings, and is expected to be more responsible. The youngest child may well be the least responsible because he/she grows up feeling able to rely on others.

4 An only child could develop independence because he/she has no one but the parents to depend on. Unlike a middle or youngest child, the only has no one to help him/her when the parents are gone.

5 Individual answers will vary.

See *General Organization and Guidelines,* page viii, in the *Introduction* for comments on **PART 2**.

PART 3

FURTHER READING, WRITING, AND DISCUSSION

Ⓐ Preparing to read

REFLECTION AND DISCUSSION (page 13)

The purpose of the exercise is for students to become familiar with some of the ideas and vocabulary of the second reading. At this point students haven't read the selection yet, so all supported answers will be welcome and helpful in preparing to read.

Ⓑ Reading for overall meaning

Answers (page 14)

Answers will vary depending on how much the students agree with the thesis of the reading and how well the couples they know fit the pattern described by the author.

Ⓔ Discussion: Critical thinking

Possible answers (page 16)

1 Opinions will vary, but most will probably agree that Forer's subject matter is more serious and her style more academic or formal. The excerpt in Part 1 is from one of two books the psychologist wrote on birth order. Withers' subject matter is lighter and perhaps more entertaining. As a magazine writer, Withers uses a style that is lively and energetic. We see this in her everyday examples, shorter sentences, and expressive vocabulary.

2 Individual answers to this question will vary according to what students think of birth-order theory. If they find it valid, it shouldn't be surprising to find that it applies to friends and co-workers, too. Forer suggests the influence of birth order is wide-ranging in one's life.

3 Individual answers to this question will vary.

....

PART 4

FOCUS ON WRITING SKILLS

Ⓑ Meeting reader expectations: Writing topic sentences

EXERCISE 2 *The main idea*

Answers (page 18)

1 Yes. The first sentence is the topic sentence: *There are obviously factors other than birth order that affect how we deal with other people.*

2 Main points of support: 1) Some societies are communal, and people other than parents are involved in raising the children; 2) Heredity plays a role in differentiating children; and 3) Our parents themselves are a big factor in what kind of people we are.

3 Individual answers will vary. However, three strong discrete points of support are usually adequate in a paragraph.

4 It is unified in that the major points of support, as well as secondary ones, support the topic sentence.

5 It is a concluding sentence for the paragraph, one that summarizes the main points for the reader.

EXERCISE 3 *Topic sentences*

Answers (page 19)

1 Both *psychology*, the topic, and the statement about it are too general. Neither would give the writer any direction in developing a paragraph.

2 *Signing up for a course* is narrow enough to be a good topic, but the statement about it is too specific; there is little more to say. Making an adjustment could result in a better topic sentence: *Registering for classes can be hectic and disappointing.*

3 Good. The topic, a boy turning eight, is narrow enough, and the statement about it can easily lead to a paragraph. The statement is likely not true of boys in most students' countries, but that is not the point here.

4 The topic, B. F. Skinner, is sufficiently narrow. The statement about the topic, however, is too general; whole books are written about the learning process.

5 Good. The topic is narrow enough; the statement about it could lead to a good paragraph about how only children learn to play by themselves.

6 Good. Both the topic and the statement about it could lead to a good paragraph. Students may argue that the statement is not true about their countries, but that is not the point here.

7 Good. The topic, *children from happy marriages,* is sufficiently narrow; the statement could lead to a good paragraph containing a discussion of reasons.

8 Both the topic and the statement about it are too general to help a student write a good paragraph.

❸ Sentence grammar: Phrases, clauses, and fragments

PHRASES AND CLAUSES

EXERCISE 4 *Adding phrases and dependent clauses to independent clauses*

Answers (page 20)

2 In Egypt relatives are more likely to live with a family *than they are in many western countries.*

3 There may be more resources *like attention and affection* for children *with other adult relatives in the household.*

4 This extended family configuration probably changes the effects *of birth order.*

5 There may be less competition *for the parents' affection* among siblings.

6 It would be surprising *to most of us,* however, *if none of the ideas about birth order were correct for Egypt.*

7 *For example,* we would still expect the oldest child to be more responsible *in comparison with his brothers and sisters.*

FRAGMENTS

EXERCISE 5 *Identifying fragments*

Answers (page 21)

  _b_ **1** Parents try to give a fair share of the family's resources to each child. In order to distribute the resources evenly.

  _a_ **2** The children themselves are not so interested in an even distribution of resources. They compete. Because each one wants as much as possible of the parents' time and attention.

  _b_ **3** Smaller children usually learn that they can compete with older ones. Despite their small size.

  _OK_ **4** Because they are smaller and weaker, younger children can usually count on the help of the parents in a dispute with siblings. Most parents will get involved.

  _b_ **5** Younger children learn to use their smallness and weakness to their advantage. They can easily become tattletales. Or even crybabies.

<u>OK</u> **6** A tattletale reports misdeeds of a sibling to parents. For example, the tattletale will say things like, "Mommy, Bobbie hit me again!"

<u>b</u> **7** A crybaby soon learns the power of tears to get what he or she wants. <u>And to win in a conflict with an older sibling.</u>

CORRECTING FRAGMENTS

EXERCISE 6 *Correcting fragments*

Answers (page 22)

1 Two only children who marry each other may have problems. <u>Because both are used to a lot of attention and approval.</u>

Two only children who marry each other may have problems because both are used to a lot of attention and approval.

2 An oldest child may find that another oldest is not a good marriage match. An oldest may be happier with an only child. <u>Or with a youngest child.</u>

An oldest may be happier with an only child or with a youngest child.

3 A youngest sister of sisters matches best with an oldest brother. <u>Who will appreciate her charm. Also tolerate her manipulation.</u>

A youngest sister of sisters matches best with an oldest brother who will appreciate her charm and tolerate her manipulation.

4 The best match for a middle child is often another middle child. <u>Since both are tactful. And normally not aggressive.</u>

The best match for a middle child is often another middle child since both are tactful and normally not aggressive.

5 <u>Although only children find it easier to make good matches.</u> There are bad matches for them. <u>Such as another only.</u>

Although only children find it easier to make good matches, there are bad matches for them, such as another only.

EXERCISE 7 *Editing for fragments*

Answers (page 23)

1 Critics of birth-order theory say that it is not scientific. <u>Because one cannot prove it. And because it is like astrology. Interesting, perhaps, but not to be taken seriously.</u> Supporters of birth-order theory admit that it alone does not determine what kind of people we are. Our parents and society, for example, are very strong influences. <u>Whether we are happy or gloomy, calm or nervous, or good-natured or bad-tempered</u>

people. However, birth order plays a role. <u>Determining the degree to which a child is</u> <u>happy, calm, and good-natured, for example.</u> It plays another role. <u>In determining how</u> <u>a child uses his or her happiness, calmness, and good-naturedness in dealing with</u> <u>other people.</u>

Sample answers

2   Critics of birth-order theory say that it is not scientific because one cannot prove it. Also, it is like astrology in that it is interesting, perhaps, but not to be taken seriously. Supporters of birth-order theory admit that it alone does not determine what kind of people we are. Our parents and society, for example, are very strong influences on whether we are happy or gloomy, calm or nervous, or good-natured or bad-tempered people. However, birth order plays a role in determining the degree to which a child is happy, calm, and good-natured, for example. It plays another role: It determines how a child uses his or her happiness, calmness, and good-naturedness in dealing with other people.

PART 5

FORMAL WRITING ASSIGNMENT

See *General Organization and Guidelines,* page xi, in the *Introduction* for additional comments on this part.

Ⓐ Writing topics (page 24)

For students who already have experience writing multi-paragraph essays, consider the following alternative topics or any others that occur to you and the students:

1 Would birth-order theory help people to find the right husband or wife in your country? Give examples of real couples for whom the theory is or is not accurate. If you decide against birth-order theory, you may want to discuss more important factors in finding the right spouse.

2 Compare/contrast two people you know in terms of birth-order theory. The people you choose should be ones for whom the theory is accurate.

Students who are not writing essays but need more work or to be challenged can be asked to write a paragraph on more than one topic.

CHAPTER 2

Matters
of the Heart

··

GENERAL COMMENTS

Like Chapter 1, Chapter 2 focuses on paragraph writing. In this chapter,
students learn to recognize patterns of organization and apply them
in developing expository paragraphs. Students also begin to practice
summarizing others' ideas as support for their own and learn to correct
run-on sentences.

Some students may already be familiar with paragraph organization
and be ready to write essays. These students may choose to look ahead
to Part 4 of Chapter 3 to prepare for an alternative formal writing
assignment in this chapter. Part 4 of Chapter 3 should be useful to
illustrate points you may want to make about form, thesis statements, and
logical assertions. Students will want to study the student model essay,
"Different Stages of Friendship" on page 71 and the *Essay Assessment
Checklist* at the end of Chapter 3 if they write an essay rather than a
paragraph.

SPECIFIC COMMENTS AND ANSWER KEY

PART 1
···

INTRODUCTION TO THE TOPIC,
READING, AND DISCUSSION

B Discussion

Answers (page 29)

1 Clearly, Esther's homesickness will continue.

2 By not letting Esther leave, Father Paul seems more interested in his work than in her
happiness. We learn he has refused her requests before.

3 Individual answers will vary.

4 Individual answers will vary.

5 Individual answers will vary.

ⓒ Preparing to read

PREVIEWING THE VOCABULARY

Answers (page 30)

1 a	**4** b	**7** c	**10** a	**13** b
2 c	**5** a	**8** c	**11** c	**14** c
3 c	**6** c	**9** c	**12** a	

ⓓ Reading for overall meaning

Answers (page 32)

At the end of the story, Esther returns to her people.

ⓔ Reading for more detail

Answers (page 35)

1 Laurence, or Esther's love for him, ended her homesickness. (Remainder of answer will vary.)

2 Esther overheard Father Paul talk Laurence out of marrying her.

3 Father Paul convinced Laurence by pointing out his own marriage plans for Laurence with a rich white girl and by frightening Laurence about the wildness and unpredictability of Indians. (Remainder of answer will vary.)

4 Esther's love for both Father Paul and Laurence turned to hatred.

5 Individual answers will vary.

6 Esther killed Laurence with poison while he slept. (Remainder of answer will vary.)

7 Individual answers will vary.

See *General Organization and Guidelines,* page viii, in the *Introduction* for comments on **PART 2**.

PART 3

FURTHER READING, WRITING, AND DISCUSSION

Ⓑ Reading for overall meaning

Answers (page 38)

In the end, there was no medicine. However, if we see the judge's advice as as a kind of medicine, then his medicine did solve the wife's problems.

Ⓔ Discussion: Critical thinking

Answers (page 40)

1 Opinions will vary, but some might cite Esther's passion as proof of her love. They may see a connection between her love and her later hatred. Others may see the Ethiopian wife's determination as a sign of deeper, truer love.

2 Individual answers will vary.

3 Individual answers will vary.

PART 4

FOCUS ON WRITING SKILLS

Ⓑ Meeting reader expectations: Patterns of organization

EXERCISE 2 *Model paragraphs: Patterns of organization*

Paragraph 1 *Examples*

Answers (page 42)

1 Yes. The first sentence is the topic sentence: *Literature gives us many examples of jealousy, but a look at daily life yields an ample supply closer at hand.*

2 Three examples are used to make the writer's point: 1) the example of the three-year-old child, 2) the wife at a party, and 3) the young computer programmer.

3 Individual answers will vary. Three good examples should be adequate to support most points, however. Students more often err on the side of giving too few examples to support a point.

4 The writer could not assume that his audience of second-language students would be familiar with the literature that might be chosen. The writer tried to find examples the audience would understand.

5 We assume the examples are hypothetical because the writer doesn't identify the people. (Remainder of answer will vary.)

Paragraph 2 *Cause and effect*

Answers (page 43)

1 The topic sentence is the third one in the paragraph: *In surveys, psychologists have discovered three personality characteristics that the very jealous have in common.* This location of the topic sentence is not the most common, but it is this way because of the introductory information the writer wanted to give before the topic sentence.

2 The writer gives three causes: 1) insecurity in relationships, 2) discrepancy between how one is and how one would like to be, and 3) too much attention to worldly items.

3 *Causes* are connected to *effects*. *Causes* answer the question "Why?" *Examples* answer the question "What?"

4 The paragraph seems complete in that the writer mentions all three of the characteristics jealous people have in common according to the surveys, and the three causes seem conclusive.

5 The conclusion reminds readers that jealousy has psychological causes inside the jealous person. The writer may feel that this somewhat unusual idea needs to be restated in a conclusion, but he may also want to reassure readers that jealousy is a *normal* human emotion. Some students may feel the paragraph is stronger without the conclusion but should be prepared to explain why an abrupt ending to a paragraph is better than a smooth one.

Paragraph 3 *Definition*

Answers (page 44)

1 The topic sentence is the third one: *Jealousy is the feeling of fear, unhappiness, or even ill will that arises when a person feels that an important relationship with someone is threatened.*

2 The definition of jealousy is the topic sentence of this paragraph.

3 The purpose here is different than the purpose in paragraph 1. Here, the writer's purpose is to define jealousy and try to make the definition clearer by speculating on the nature of jealousy – whether biological or economic. To make his definition clearer, he does give examples of economic causes of jealousy, however.

Paragraph 4 *Comparison and contrast*

Answers (page 44)

1 The topic sentence is the first one: *The terms* jealousy *and* envy *are often used in place of each other, but there is a basic distinction to be made between them.* The writer's purpose is to contrast jealousy and envy.

2 Examples of envy are envy of a neighbor's car and of a classmate's high test score. Examples of jealousy are a jealous husband and a jealous child. The examples help achieve the writer's purpose: to contrast jealousy and envy. They help the reader understand the differences between them.

3 *Envy* is for something we don't have; *jealousy* is for something we have but might lose. Envy is not accepted by society, whereas jealousy is.

4 (1) Point-by-point organization.

5 Possible conclusion: Envy and jealousy are similar, yet different, ideas.

Paragraph 5 *Narrative*

Answers (page 45)

1 Individual answers will vary.

2 The topic sentence is the first one: *The first time I remember feeling jealous was many years ago when I was three or four.*

3 *My father, too, might like the pictures, but I thought he was sleeping* seems a little irrelevant until we realize that the writer's misunderstanding about his father's whereabouts is important to the narrative.

4 The events, in chronological order, are: 1) choosing crayons, 2) finishing the picture and desiring to show it to his mother, 3) going into the kitchen, 4) finding his mother and father kissing, 5) failing at attempt to interrupt, 6) running to his room.

Paragraph 6 *Description*

Answers (page 45)

1 The purpose of the description is to paint a picture of a jealous person with words. The writer describes a jealous person's feelings (*shame, anger, emptiness, insecurity*). The writer gives examples of what John did that *show* us his jealousy. However, the paragraph is not a chronological story as a narrative would be.

2 In a picture of a jealous person, we see shame, anger, emptiness, and insecurity.

3 Some details appeal to our senses of feeling, sight, and even hearing: *feeling anger building in his head, like a bomb about to explode, a soft sigh of disbelief, a look of confusion.*

4 Possible topic sentence: *We can recognize a jealous person by looking at the person's feelings.*

Paragraph 7 *Classification*

Answers (page 46)

1 In an example paragraph, the writer chooses a few good examples from many. In a classification, the writer tries to include all possible instances of something in a few categories.

2 Individual answers will vary.

3 The first sentence is an introductory one to help the reader better understand the topic sentence, which expresses the main idea of the paragraph. The topic sentence is the second sentence: *All cases of jealousy probably fall into one of four categories.* This might seem abrupt if the writer didn't separate "feeling" from "cause."

4 Individual answers will vary.

Ⓒ Sentence grammar: Correcting run-on sentences

RUN-ON SENTENCES

EXERCISE 3 *Recognizing run-on sentences*

Answers (page 47)

1 RO		**4** C	
2 C		**5** C	
3 RO		**6** RO	

EXERCISE 4 *Separating run-on sentences*

Answers (page 48)

1 Communication does not happen only through words; it happens through actions and gestures, too.

2 A compliment usually communicates appreciation; criticism can be destructive.

3 Communicating with another includes admitting when you feel low or lonely. Not sharing these feelings creates distance.

4 It is important to accept what another says as significant and real. It may not seem important to you but probably is to the speaker.

5 Sometimes good communication means respecting another's silence. We must accept that people sometimes need quiet to solve problems.

EXERCISE 5 *Using transition words*

Answers (page 49)

1 Some people feel that total honesty is essential in a loving relationship. *However,* others feel it is dangerous to be completely honest.

2 One writer feels that good lies lead to a good marriage. *In other words,* a person should lie in order not to hurt the spouse's feelings.

3 Another writer recommends always telling the truth; *in this way,* trust is created between the two spouses.

4 Sometimes a small lie can have serious consequences. *For example,* a husband who tells his wife he likes a meal that he hates may end up eating that meal over and over again.

5 Eventually, the lying husband will probably explode in anger; *then,* he may say something very hurtful about his wife's cooking.

6 Perhaps the simple truth, told tactfully in the beginning, would have been better. *Thus,* the wife would not have made the problem meal again.

7 The problem of honesty in relationships applies to all of us almost every time we speak; *therefore,* it is an issue that is worth thinking about.

EXERCISE 6 *Using coordinating conjunctions*

Answers (page 50)

1 There are two qualities that are destructive to a loving relationship, *and* not surprisingly, they are the opposite aspects of the essential qualities we have already looked at.

2 Lack of communication is at the top of the "destructive" list, *so* we can see how important communication is to a healthy loving relationship.

3 Selfishness can eventually destroy a loving relationship, *but* an unforgiving nature can make love disappear very quickly. (*Yet* also works here in place of *but*.)

4 A lack of trust is a problem, *for* distrust can weaken any relationship.

5 A perfectionist can make the other person feel incompetent, *so* the other person may feel it is pointless trying to please the perfectionist.

EXERCISE 7 *Using subordinating conjunctions*

Answers (page 51)

1 *Even though* acceptance and a sense of humor aren't the qualities most people think of first, they are very important qualities in a loving relationship.

2 *If* we really love someone, it means we love the person as they are, not as we would like them to be.

3 *Because* not everything in life turns out the way we want, a sense of humor about life is a way of accepting what comes our way.

4 A sense of humor can make us feel rich and happy *even though* it is not the result of how many possessions we have.

5 *Because* some people take themselves and life too seriously, they can become easily disappointed when things turn out differently than they expect.

6 We can say that we see the humor in life *if* we are quick to laugh at ourselves and the difficulties life brings.

7 A relationship can become boring and predictable *unless* the people in the relationship have a sense of humor.

EXERCISE 8 *Editing for run-on sentences*

Sample answers (page 51)

Some people are probably more successful in their relationships / they have the qualities essential to loving relationships. The lack of these qualities is probably the cause of many problems we have with other people / many of us would benefit from developing those qualities we don't have. For example, many people get married and divorced over and over again / others don't get along with coworkers on the job. Perhaps their lives would be easier if they were better at communication / if they were more honest about their feelings.

Some people are probably more successful in their relationships *because* they have the qualities essential to loving relationships. The lack of these qualities is probably the cause of many problems we have with other people. *Therefore,* many of us would benefit from developing those qualities we don't have. For example, many people get married and divorced over and over again. *In addition,* others don't get along with coworkers on the job. Perhaps their lives would be easier if they were better at communication and if they were more honest about their feelings.

PART 5

FORMAL WRITING ASSIGNMENT

See *General Organization and Guidelines,* page xi, in the *Introduction* for additional comments on this part.

Ⓐ Writing topics (page 52)

Here are some essay topics for students who are already familiar with paragraph organization:

1 Is a good relationship easy to achieve? Focus on one kind of relationship: a couple, a parent and child, or two siblings.

2 Do men and women express love in the same way? Or does gender influence the expression of love?

Friendship

....

Chapter 3 introduces the essay and shows the relationship between a paragraph and an essay. It discusses thesis statements and the importance of making logical assertions in them. Part 4 deals with subject-verb agreement.

Students sometimes write weaker paragraphs when they begin writing essays because of the pressures of writing a longer assignment. Therefore, you may want to stress the importance of maintaining attention to paragraphs while developing a longer piece of writing. The *Essay Assessment Checklist* at the end of the chapter reminds students of these major points.

SPECIFIC COMMENTS AND ANSWER KEY

PART 1

....

INTRODUCTION TO THE TOPIC, READING, AND DISCUSSION

ⓒ Preparing to read

PREVIEWING THE VOCABULARY

Answers (page 57)

1 c	4 c	7 b	10 a	13 c
2 c	5 a	8 c	11 c	
3 a	6 c	9 b	12 a	

ⓓ Reading for overall meaning

Answers (page 59)

The study shows friendship is alive and well. (It concludes that people's descriptions of friendships, their beliefs about them, and their ideas about the rules governing friendship are consistent with each other. The research found few contradictions.)

ⓔ Reading for more detail

Answers (page 62)

1 Social critics, citing the high mobility rate in the United States, expected the *Psychology Today* report to reflect the self-indulgence and lack of commitment in U.S. society that they currently write about. Somehow, despite the impersonality and anomie of modern city life, friendship in the United States is alive and well.

2 The five important qualities are 1) loyalty, 2) the ability to keep confidences, 3) warmth, 4) affection, and 5) supportiveness. (Remainder of answer will vary.)

3 The two reasons given for ending a friendship are 1) feeling betrayed and 2) discovering that a friend had very different views on important matters. (Remainder of answer will vary.)

4 Having intimate talks, helping out a friend, and turning to a friend for help are the three activities most characteristic among friends. (Remainder of answer will vary.)

5 The rules of friendship include friends confiding in each other by sharing intimate aspects, both good and bad, of their personal lives and feelings. The rules of friendship also involve the right to ask for help. (Remainder of answer will vary.)

6 Most Americans (90 percent) think a person should not help a friend commit suicide.

7 Individual answers will vary.

See *General Organization and Guidelines*, page viii, in the *Introduction* for comments on PART 2.

PART 3

···

FURTHER READING, WRITING, AND DISCUSSION

ⓑ Reading for overall meaning

Answers (page 65)

We cannot know for sure, but most students who have read this selection have felt that the two women became real friends.

E Discussion: Critical thinking (page 67)

Individual answers will vary. Note that in the third question, "Birds of a feather flock together" is said of friends (or couples) who are similar, or who have a lot in common. They are attracted to each other because they are similar. "Opposites attract" has just the opposite message: We are attracted to those who are different from us.

PART 4
....
FOCUS ON WRITING SKILLS

B Meeting reader expectations: The essay and logical assertions

EXERCISE 2 *Parts of the essay*

Answers (page 69)

2 d   **5** f

3 a   **6** e

4 c

EXERCISE 3 *Student essay on friendship*

Answers (page 71)

1 The essay contains five paragraphs.

2 Individual answers will vary. Ms. Kumazawa uses the example of an exceptional friendship to move toward her thesis statement. This friendship, by not following the usual "stages" of friendship, gives the reader a perspective on what she will say about friendship. To many, this approach will seem logical. Her thesis statement: *The process of making friends can be divided into three stages: new friends and acquaintances, true friends, and best friends.*

3 Yes, each body paragraph has its own main idea. The second body paragraph (on true friendship) may strike students as being underdeveloped. Each body paragraph concentrates on one "stage" of friendship as mentioned in the thesis statement.

4 Ms. Kumazawa does not remind the reader of the three stages, but she does reiterate that people have different kinds of friends. She lets the reader see the significance of friendship to life in general when she points out the happiness, joy, and humanity it brings people. (Remainder of answer will vary.)

5 Individual answers will vary.

EXERCISE 4 *Topic sentence or thesis statement?*

This exercise has two goals: to help students distinguish general topics from more specific ones and to get them used to taking measure of how much they have to say on a topic. The benefit of the exercise comes from the thinking that students do rather than the initial choices they make.

Sample answers and comments (page 72)

1 Essay: No single paragraph could do justice to this contrast.

2 Paragraph/Essay: Certainly, books are written on the topic of friendships between men and women, but these often include research on the topic and/or expert opinion. Students could easily cover the topic in a paragraph. Some might argue, with reason, that they could develop a whole essay on the topic. If they do, ask them what support paragraphs they would use.

3 Paragraph: Students could use the reading or their own knowledge to write a well-developed paragraph. An attempt at an essay would lead most students into repeating the same information in successive paragraphs because the topic is limited.

4 Paragraph/Essay: Students should be able to write a good paragraph on the qualities, probably by giving an example of each quality. More mature students will be able to limit the qualities to two or three important ones that can be discussed at more length in an essay.

5 Paragraph/Essay: Using only the information in the reading, students could write a good paragraph. Drawing on their own experiences, they could expand the topic into an essay.

6 Paragraph: This topic is well-suited to a narrative paragraph. Were it expanded into an essay, the writing would probably become diluted – a one paragraph narrative diluted into three paragraphs.

7 Paragraph/Essay: This could be treated succinctly in a paragraph. With thought and effort, it could also be expanded into an essay by many students.

8 Paragraph/Essay: Students should be able to write a well-developed paragraph from their own experiences or by using information from the readings. An essay will require much more thinking to be more than a very long paragraph stretched out into the form of an essay.

9 Paragraph: A good paragraph could be developed using examples or even a narrative. An attempt to expand it into an essay, say, by devoting three paragraphs to three examples, could easily result in using major evidence to make a minor point.

10 Essay: To be informative and convincing, this topic would require an essay – and substantial thinking by the writer. The topic itself – *different kinds of friends* – is limited. However, the statement made about it – *for different parts of our lives* – will take thought and explanation to match with the *different kinds of friends*.

EXERCISE 5 *Logical assertions*

Note: Reasons *a* and *c* on page 74 are deceivingly similar. The difference between reasons *a, b, c, d* and a logical assertion (*LA*) is illustrated in these statements:

a. Soccer is the world's best sport. (subjective assertion)

b. Soccer is played by more people than any other sport in the world. (fact)

c. I like soccer better than other sports. (question of taste)

d. Soccer will surpass football in popularity in the United States in the next century. (unverifiable)

LA: Soccer is the world's most popular sport for a number of reasons.

Answers (page 74)

1 a

2 a

3 b

4 LA   This statement sounds suspiciously like a subjective assertion, and many may see it that way, but it does express an opinion about happiness that a reader can disagree with, and logical support is necessary to convince the reader.

5 LA

6 a

7 d

8 LA

9 c

10 LA

Ⓓ Sentence grammar: Subject-verb agreement

EXERCISE 6 *Subject-verb agreement: Guidelines 1 and 2*

Answers (page 76)

1 A friend *accepts* our weaknesses, whereas relatives often *pretend* that we don't have any weaknesses.

2 Sharing confidences with friends and trusting them to be discreet *are* important requirements of friendship.

3 Loyalty, or an unspoken agreement to remain faithful and supportive, *is* more often expected in friendship than in kinship.

4 A <u>cousin</u> and a <u>brother</u> never *stop* being relatives, but a <u>friend</u> sometimes *does* stop being a friend.

5 A <u>friend</u>, to deepen the friendly relations, *shares* his or her deepest feelings with you.

6 A <u>relative</u>, especially a close one, very likely *knows* how you are feeling without having to ask.

EXERCISE 7 *Subject-verb agreement: Guidelines 3 and 4*

Answers (page 76)

1 <u>People</u> who *know* only your good side *don't* know all of you.

2 <u>Being honest about negative feelings</u>, which *includes* saying that you have been hurt, *lets* a friend get to know you better.

3 There *are* <u>a number of habits</u> that can keep a friendship from growing.

4 <u>The tendency to "keep score,"</u> which *means* comparing what one gives to what one receives in a friendship, is a bad habit.

5 Keeping score in <u>friendships</u> that *are* important to you may harm the relationships.

6 <u>Those people</u> who *have* trouble accepting others' generosity *need* to remember how happy they are to help a friend.

EXERCISE 8 *Subject-verb agreement: Guidelines 5 and 6*

Answers (page 78)

1 An introvert is <u>someone</u> who *is* more interested in her or his own thoughts and feelings than in <u>something</u> that *is* outside herself or himself.

2 Everyone *recognizes* extroverts: <u>people</u> who *like* to be with others and to attract attention.

3 <u>An introvert and an extrovert</u> both *need* friends as <u>everyone</u> *does*.

4 Neither the introvert nor the extrovert *is* happy without knowing that he or <u>she</u> *has* friends.

5 <u>Extroverts</u> *are* probably better at making friends because almost <u>everything</u> about them *is* "friendly."

6 Neither big parties nor <u>a very public job</u> *is* attractive to an <u>introvert</u>, who *prefers* quieter surroundings.

7 On the other hand, either a party or <u>another place</u> with lots of people *appeals* to extroverts.

8 <u>Most of what</u> *is* mentioned here *comes* from research, but <u>all of it</u> *is* easy to observe among people that you know.

9 At some time in his or her life, every <u>introvert</u> probably *wishes* to be more extroverted.

10 Truth told, no <u>extrovert</u> *has* been hurt by thinking quietly about life, which <u>all of us</u> *need* to do at least occasionally.

EXERCISE 9 *Subject-verb agreement: Guidelines 7 and 8*

Answers (page 79)

1 <u>A young audience</u> *is* often more enthusiastic than an older one.

2 He found that <u>physics</u> *was* more difficult for him than he had thought it would be.

3 <u>Economics and mathematics</u> *require* a certain amount of concentration to understand.

4 From what they said on TV, the <u>government</u> *is* going to announce tax reforms soon.

5 <u>Politics</u> *has* never made much sense to me.

6 The <u>news</u> about the earthquakes *was* quite discouraging.

7 The <u>two pieces</u> of news John shared with us *were* both distressing.

EXERCISE 10 *Editing for subject-verb agreement*

Answers (page 79)

For me loyalty is an important part of friendship. A loyal friend is true and faithful to me. Loyalty to friends *does* not mean that my friends should support me when I am wrong, however. Sometimes people *support* friends who *have* lied or been dishonest to others. This kind of support is not loyalty. A loyal friend would support my decision to go away to school, even if it meant our separation. A loyal friend supports decisions and actions that honestly *benefit* you, even if the friend *loses* something in the process.

PART 5

FORMAL WRITING ASSIGNMENT

This will be the first time that most of your students will be writing a full essay, so you may want to provide a little extra help if they seem overwhelmed. You might do this by allowing a little extra time for section B, *Generating Ideas: Mind Mapping,* and section C, *Expanding Your Point of View: Group Discussion.* This may also be the right time for informal writing conferences. Let students work on their first drafts in class while you move around the room answering questions. (See Part 5 of *General Organization and Guidelines,* page xi, in the *Introduction* for more ideas about writing conferences.) For starters, you will probably want to make sure that each student has a clear, logical thesis statement on which to base his or her essay. All else depends on that crucial part of the essay.

Live to Work or Work to Live?

Chapter 4 continues to focus on the essay, emphasizing the introduction and conclusion. With the pressures of writing a longer essay, students sometimes neglect the introduction, reducing it to a sentence or two including their thesis statement. They need to be aware that an introduction functions as more than a vehicle for the thesis statement; it should catch the reader's attention and can give background information the reader will need in order to follow the essay.

In a hurry to finish, students will often write a very brief conclusion that can seem abrupt to a reader. Students will quickly understand that a conclusion can be used to summarize their main points. Harder to grasp is the notion that a good conclusion lets the reader know how the writer's ideas are significant in the writer's life, or how they might be used by the reader.

In addition to the focus on the introduction and conclusion, *Sentence Grammar* in Part 4 takes another look at summarization and practices adding coherence to writing.

PART 1

INTRODUCTION TO THE TOPIC, READING, AND DISCUSSION

ⓑ Discussion

Answers (page 86)

1 Answers may vary; however, the grasshopper's singing is support for his being more content than the ant.

2 In the winter, the grasshopper is no longer content because he has nothing to eat.

3 Individual answers will vary.

4 Individual answers will vary.

ⓒ Preparing to read

NOTES ON THE READING

Answers (page 87)

__T__ **1 philander** (to have sexual relationships outside one's marriage)

__G__ **2** a life of industry and **thrift** (spending money carefully)

__T__ **3 promises of amendment** (promises to change one's behavior)

__T__ **4 idle** (lazy, avoiding work)

__G__ **5** a small income from **gilt-edged securities** (safe investments)

__T__ **6 blackmail** (threaten to act a certain way unless you are paid money)

__T__ **7 end in the gutter** (end up poor, living in the street)

PREVIEWING THE VOCABULARY

Answers (page 87)

1 c	4 b	7 a	10 c	13 a
2 b	5 c	8 b	11 b	
3 a	6 c	9 c	12 b	

D Reading for overall meaning

Answers (page 90)

The message in Maugham's story is different from the message in Aesop's fable. It is, in fact, the opposite message in that the idle Tom is rewarded in the end and the industrious George feels miserable.

E Reading for more detail

Answers (page 93)

1 George didn't like that his brother Tom was the black sheep of the family: the one who quit working, abandoned his wife, borrowed money, and blackmailed his brother. (Remainder of answer will vary.)

2 Tom was charming and could usually borrow from friends and from George. After George "washed his hands of him," Tom would blackmail his brother by embarrassing him — as he did when he took jobs as a barman or driver.

3 George was upset because he thought he would finally be vindicated for all his hard work and sacrifice. He also thought that Tom would be punished, or at least suffer, for his carefree life. But Tom didn't suffer; he was nicely rewarded in the end. (Remainder of answer will vary.)

4 At the end of the story, it is obvious that the narrator likes Tom, is charmed by him, and probably approves of his behavior.

5 The message in Maugham's story seems to tell us that we should enjoy life and not work too much — the opposite of the message in the fable. Students may be interested in this British saying, which applies to George in the story: "All work and no play makes Jack a dull boy."

6 Individual answers will vary.

See *General Organization and Guidelines,* page viii, in the *Introduction* for comments on PART 2.

PART 3

FURTHER READING, WRITING, AND DISCUSSION

Ⓑ Reading for overall meaning

Answers (page 96)

Answers will vary as students will like and dislike different letters. If you choose to discuss the reading in class, the two questions could be a good way to start the discussion.

Ⓔ Discussion: Critical thinking (page 99)

All four questions ask for students' opinions, so answers will vary. Some students may object to question 1. Perhaps a father's responsibilities are different from a mother's or just less palpable. In question 3, a point not taken up in the reading but that may influence how balanced work makes us feel is this: What kind of work are we talking about? A worker in a car factory might not feel the same satisfaction or sense of fulfillment from work that a doctor, teacher, or plumber does.

PART 4

FOCUS ON WRITING SKILLS

Ⓑ Meeting reader expectations: Introductions and conclusions

Answers (page 100)

1 Individual answers will vary.

2 Indirectly, the fable gives an idea of what the story is about. Some may argue that the fable is misleading as an introduction because its message is the opposite of Maugham's message in the story. But both the fable and the story deal with attitudes toward work and life.

3 The writer lets us know what he thinks of the way the story ends. Though he may feel sorry for George, he is happy for Tom. We would not get the author's full message without this conclusion; we would only know the story ended differently from the fable.

4 Both the introduction and conclusion are relatively short (15 lines and 5 lines, respectively, out of 120 total). Students coming from a writing tradition that requires long, slow, careful introductions that often amount to one half of the length of the written piece will benefit from noticing the short, effective introduction used by Maugham and favored by English rhetoric. Students who tend to write very short introductions merely to announce the thesis statement should benefit from the interesting way Maugham begins his story.

5 This may not be immediately obvious, but Maugham goes from the general (a fable most people know) to the specific (two brothers we don't know). It's not a point worth dwelling on but does tie in to the discussion of introductions and conclusions in Part 4.

EXERCISE 2 *Student essay*

Answers (page 102)

1 Mr. Shchegolev gives the background necessary for the reader to understand his point. Without a discussion of the traditional view of work, Igor's less conventional view would be harder to follow.

2 Individual answers will vary. The fact that the writer disagrees with Aesop will stand out and spark interest for many readers. Many will be interested in following how the writer goes beyond a conventional conception of work.

3 The writer's thesis is that work and labor are different. It appears in a thesis statement at the end of the introduction: *Life is more complicated than an Aesop fable because there is a big difference between labor and work.*

4 Answers will vary as to how effectively Mr. Shchegolev has developed his thesis, but most should be impressed by how he has incorporated ideas from the fable and the story as well as another reading he has done; he also uses three famous men as examples. He explains that labor is something we have to do to survive; work is something we are moved or inspired to do, i.e., a creative endeavor.

5 Yankelovich's reasons for working: 1) as a way to exist, 2) as a way to improve one's level of life, and 3) as a moral necessity. Most readers will probably agree with these reasons as they are logical and conventional. We might conclude that the reasons are effective support because they reach the audience. The reasons become more compelling when the writer tells us they are only part of the story, that they explain labor but not creative work.

6 The writer briefly lists the main points of support again for the readers and points out how the readers might use this information: by being more creative and not merely doing labor in their lives.

7 Answers will vary, but students should leave the exercise understanding that the introduction and conclusion in this essay are of conventional length for an essay written in English.

8 It may not be immediately obvious, but the essay does follow the general-to-specific-to-general diagram. Mr. Shchegolev begins by referring to Aesop's fable and the Maugham story, with which all of his readers are familiar at this point. He moves toward his specific thesis at the end of the introduction and develops that thesis. In his conclusion, he reminds us of his major points and leaves this point as he moves to a more general one: how we might apply what he has to say about work and labor to be more creative.

● Sentence grammar: Adding coherence

COHESIVE DEVICES

EXERCISE 3 *Adding coherence to a paragraph*

Answers (page 106)

A researcher helps explain a problem that many workers complain of. Most workers want to do their best. [1] (a) *However,* they do not work as hard as they could [2] (b) *because* they feel that others receive the benefits of their hard work. [3] (c) The researcher doesn't see this attitude as a sign of a weak work ethic. [4] (a) *Rather,* he feels the attitude would change if workers made more of the decisions that affect their work. There is a message for managers in this research. Managers need to allow workers to express their needs, [5] (c) *and* they need to listen to what workers say.

EXERCISE 4 *More practice adding coherence to paragraphs*

Answers (page 106)

Some companies do actually try to address their workers' needs and suggestions. [1] (b) *For instance,* a few companies offer day-care facilities for workers' children. [2] (c) *That way,* workers can have more contact with their children during the day. The workers' minds are freed from worries about their children [3] (b), *so* theoretically, they work better. [4] (a) Some other companies offer their employees flexible working hours. Workers can begin and finish work at times they choose. [5] (c) *Of course,* they still have to put in the required number of hours. [6] (a) *Therefore,* if they begin work late, they have to stay late. Other companies are listening to workers' suggestions about improving efficiency in the factory or office. [7] (b) *Even though* managers still make the final decisions, they have begun to consider the workers' input when making those decisions.

EXERCISE 5 *Editing for coherence*

Sample answers (page 108)

English, like other languages, has conflicting sayings about important matters like love, friendship, and work. *For example,* in English we say about work, "Never put off till tomorrow what you can do today." The message is that one can and should always work more—at least until all the work is done. *On the other hand,* in English we *also* have this proverb: "All work and no play makes Jack a dull boy." The advice is not to work too much *because* life without recreation makes one an uninteresting person. How is it that the language has two sayings that give opposite messages? We can assume that work is important to native English speakers *because* they respect it a lot—perhaps too much. The second saying may be a kind of safety valve *since* it warns people against going too far in following the advice of the first saying.

PART 5

FORMAL WRITING ASSIGNMENT

See *General Organization and Guidelines,* page xi, in the *Introduction* for additional comments on this part.

● Expanding your point of view: Interview (page 110)

Students in an EFL setting can interview people from their own countries to expand their points of view. Even if they are conversing in their own language, they will benefit from another person's point of view.

Out of Courtesy

The topic of Chapter 5 is courtesy. If people do something "out of courtesy," they are acting in a polite way, considering others and their feelings. It is easy to respond to the topic of courtesy with platitudes about how the world will be better if people are just "nice" to each other. Teachers of students from other cultures, however, realize that the question of courtesy is much more complicated than such simple assertions imply. Students have on occasion unknowingly been impolite; they, in turn, have undoubtedly found the behavior of teachers and students from other cultures bizarre, if not downright rude.

The writing topics in this lesson require a lot of thinking because they are topics most people do not normally think about in more than a superficial way. There is also an ethnocentric tendency in most people to believe that their own country's etiquette could, if not should, be universal.

Chapter 5 also introduces outlining as a first step in drafting. Although outlining is often seen as the antithesis of free writing and other progressive means of stimulating thought, it nonetheless is an important skill that can help students later when they write exams and papers in their fields.

When writing, students usually start with information and ideas. What they need to do is organize their ideas. They need to decide which are the main ideas, which are secondary ones, and which ones should be excluded. They need to decide the order in which they will present the ideas in the essay. An outline helps them make these decisions. Therefore, this chapter teaches outlining as a useful skill. Outlining is not and should not be thought of as a way to generate ideas.

In *Sentence Grammar,* in Part 4, students practice adding variety to the types of sentences they write by looking at simple, compound, and complex sentences in detail.

PART 1

INTRODUCTION TO THE TOPIC, READING, AND DISCUSSION

ⓒ Preparing to read

PREVIEWING THE VOCABULARY

Answers (page 115)

1 b	**4** c	**7** b	**10** b	**13** a
2 c	**5** a	**8** b	**11** b	**14** c
3 c	**6** a	**9** c	**12** a	

ⓓ Reading for overall meaning

Answers (page 117)

Good manners are a matter of how we look at, or regard, other people as Dr. Peale points out in line 80 in the last paragraph.

ⓔ Reading for more detail

Answers (page 119)

1 Individual answers will vary. The three "basic ingredients" referred to in this question are 1) a sense of justice, 2) empathy with others, and 3) the capacity to treat all people alike.

2 Individual answers will vary.

3 Individual answers will vary. The three ways of improving manners referred to in this question are 1) practicing courtesy, 2) thinking in a courteous way, and 3) being able to accept courtesy.

4 Individual answers will vary.

5 Individual answers will vary.

See *General Organization and Guidelines,* page viii, in the *Introduction* for comments on **PART 2**.

PART 3
....
FURTHER READING, WRITING, AND DISCUSSION

Ⓐ Preparing to read (page 121)

To save time, it's often tempting for a teacher to skip a section here or there. The exercise in this section introduces a lot of the difficult vocabulary from the second reading, and although it will take time to do, it will save time in the long run.

Ⓑ Reading for overall meaning

Answers (page 122)

McCullough does not give us an easy formula for telling the difference. He concedes that it is sometimes hard to tell the difference between a white lie and a more serious one, but he encourages us to be committed to honesty even though we must stretch the truth at times.

Ⓔ Discussion: Critical thinking

Answers (page 125)

1 Most readers should agree that Dr. Peale would wholeheartedly approve of McCullough's ideas on white lies. Both writers seem to support telling a white lie out of courtesy, that is, out of consideration for another person's feelings.

2 Individual answers will vary.

3 Mark Twain's quote about lying makes one think of another saying on the subject: "Liars need to have very good memories." The idea in both sayings is that a lie lives a long time and will probably lead to other lies in support of the first lie, so the liar needs to keep track of what has been said.

4 Individual answers will vary. Students are sometimes tempted to go for a pat, general answer. Teachers will want to be wary of platitudes that trivialize the discussion, however. An intelligent discussion of the universality of manners may well end with the students not being completely sure of how they feel. This is a question that likely will require a lot more thought from students before a satisfactory answer comes. They will have that opportunity in Part 5 if they choose to write on this topic.

PART 4

FOCUS ON WRITING SKILLS

Ⓐ Meeting reader expectations: Outlining

EXERCISE 1 *Completing an outline*

Answers (page 126)

Thesis: Life's difficulties would be minimized if people were more courteous to each other.

I. Basic ingredients of good manners

    A. Justice

    B. *Empathy*

    C. *Capacity to treat all people alike*

II. Three ways to improve one's manners

    A. Practice courtesy

        1. *Concentrate on one area at a time*

        2. Don't let others' bad manners make you rude

    B. *Think in a courteous way*

    C. Be able to accept courtesy

Conclusion: Politeness is the golden rule in action.

EXERCISE 3 *A student essay*

Answers (page 129)

1 The last sentence of the introduction expresses Ms. Navarro's thesis: *Perhaps because all cultures are equally concerned about their children's manners, we find many more similarities than differences in the way Mexicans and Americans teach children the golden rule.*

2 She wrote four support paragraphs: manners that parents teach their children for use 1) at home, 2) at school, 3) with neighbors, and 4) with strangers.

3 As teachers, we hope students will agree that the paper is well organized. Each paragraph supports the thesis. The order of the paragraphs follows the chronology in which the manners are taught: first at home, then for use at school, then with neighbors, and finally with strangers. The reader can easily follow the logic of this organization. (The issue of main ideas and secondary ones might best be answered by how easy or difficult it is for students to outline paragraph 4 later in the exercise.)

4 Each body paragraph supports her thesis in that it points to the similarities (and occasionally differences) in how Mexican and U.S. parents impart the golden rule to their children.

5 Her goal in the conclusion stresses the similarities between the two cultures in their common concern to teach manners to children despite some differences that do, in fact, stand out.

I. The golden rule as it applies to neighbors is different in Mexico from in the United States.

  A. Mexicans *normally offer help when a new family comes to a neighborhood.*

    1. *They offer help in moving.*

    2. *They lend equipment like ladders.*

    3. *Some will even offer food.*

  B. Americans *apply the golden rule by not getting in the way.*

    1. *They make friends and offer support later.*

    2. *They stay out of the way in the beginning.*

      a. *Americans may be more independent and expect others to be.*

      b. *People move more often in the United States.*

Conclusion: *Neighbors are more likely to become friends in Mexico than in the United States.*

ⓒ Sentence grammar: Sentence variety

EXERCISE 4 *Distinguishing compound from simple sentences*

Answers (page 130)

1 S	4 S	7 S
2 C	5 S	8 C
3 C	6 C	

EXERCISE 5 *Writing compound sentences*

Sample answers (page 131)

1 Did they treat you courteously, or *were they rude to you?*

2 The students respect that teacher, for *she is patient and always prepared for class.*

3 I wanted to tell the truth, yet *I was afraid of how you would react to it.*

4 *I was afraid of hurting my mother's feelings*, so I told a white lie.

5 *They were eager to help me*, but I was suspicious of their motives.

6 *Justice is one ingredient of good manners*, and another is empathy.

7 *To be polite in the United States, you shouldn't fail to look your interlocutor in the eye*, nor should you fail to return a person's phone call.

8 *Mr. and Mrs. Green treat everyone, including their children, courteously*, so their children will probably have very good manners.

9 *Be careful what you think of other people*, for the thoughts in your mind determine the kind of person you are.

10 *Unfortunately, he isn't very considerate*, nor is he very tactful.

EXERCISE 6 *Writing complex sentences*

Sample answers (page 132)

1 *I didn't retaliate in kind* even though John's rude remark made me angry.

2 *I have not been able to trust Jason* since he lied to me last year.

3 Whenever someone is rude to me, *I try not to be rude in return, but it's difficult.*

4 *Nick gets along well with people at work* because he is considerate of others.

5 *I make a point of treating people with courtesy* so that they will treat me courteously, too.

6 If a person's bad manners bother you, *it may be best just to tolerate the person's unpleasant behavior.*

7 Although I try to think in a courteous way, *I sometimes find myself thinking vengefully.*

8 *People with good manners respond politely* even when they are treated discourteously.

9 If people practice courtesy, *it will eventually become a habit.*

10 Because Mr. Vann is suspicious of others' motives, *he can't really accept their good will or friendly gestures.*

EXERCISE 7 *Distinguishing simple, compound, and complex sentences*

Answers (page 132)

1 S	4 S	7 CX	10 S
2 C	5 S	8 CX	
3 CX	6 C	9 C	

EXERCISE 8 *Editing rambling sentences for sentence variety*

Sample answers (page 133)

When the telephone rang, I answered and heard the voice of my wife's best friend, Gladys. Her voice was so sweet and sugary *that* I knew she thinks I'm a jerk. *However,* that's all right because I can't stand her either. *Because* my wife was out, I had to talk to Gladys. She said she had invited my wife and me to dinner on Friday, but my wife wasn't sure if I was free. Gladys was now calling again; *to tell the truth,* I would rather watch basketball on TV and not eat than spend time with her and her boring husband. *However,* I said, "We'd be glad to come to dinner. I look forward to seeing you and Ted on Friday." Yes, I lied, but it wasn't a bad lie because it's the kind you tell to make social relationships smoother. *Although* the lie hid my feelings, it also protected a larger truth–that my wife really will look forward to the evening. She loves Gladys, and, *furthermore,* Gladys' life is full of problems right now. I love my wife and want to make her happy, so in the interest of this larger truth, lying was the courteous thing to do.

PART 5
··
FORMAL WRITING ASSIGNMENT

See *General Organization and Guidelines,* page xi, in the *Introduction* for additional comments on this part.

Ⓐ Writing topics (page 135)

Students may find it difficult to write on topic 1 if they have not lived in an English-speaking country. The student essay in this chapter is successful because Ms. Navarro has insights from experience in both cultures. Likewise, topic 3 may be too abstract for students who have lived only in one country.

Questions of Right and Wrong

GENERAL COMMENTS

Chapter 6 takes up a topic that should be both interesting and challenging to students: questions of right and wrong and what a person's moral duty is. Students should find the two readings in the chapter compelling and useful as they prepare to write a slightly different essay in this chapter: a persuasive essay for or against one of three propositions dealing with moral questions. As in other chapters, if students are not enthusiastic about the topics given, encourage them to generate ones that are more attractive to them. Environmental issues are mentioned in the first reading, and an environmental topic might be a good alternative writing topic. One word of caution: Any new topics should be stated as propositions that a writer can be *for* or *against*. A proposition for or against something lends itself to a panel discussion, the form that *Generating Ideas: Panel Discussion* in Part 5 takes in this chapter.

Sentence Grammar in Part 4 deals with consistency in tense, person, number, and tone. The model essay is written by the author rather than by a student; students may enjoy "turning the tables" on a teacher when they evaluate the essay.

··

INTRODUCTION TO THE TOPIC, READING, AND DISCUSSION

ⓒ Preparing to read

PREVIEWING THE VOCABULARY

Answers (page 141)

1 c	**4** a	**7** c	**10** a
2 b	**5** b	**8** a	**11** a
3 c	**6** c	**9** c	

ⓓ Reading for overall meaning

Answers (page 143)

Shapiro doesn't come out and say it directly, but we infer that he is not completely comfortable with his father's decision of years ago. Indeed, the discomfort is probably what prompted him to write the piece. One almost gets the feeling he is trying to rationalize his father's lack of action by comparing it to the world's seeming lack of concern for the suffering of many people. Some students may disagree; they should point to places in the text that support their position.

ⓔ Reading for more detail

Answers (page 146)

1 We conclude from a number of clues that the writer's family is comfortable, well off: *the expensive Winnebago, even if rented rather than owned; the father's reliance on charge cards even if it meant he paid more for gas; the father's profession as a doctor.*

2 Individual answers will vary. For many, the most frightening element is the screaming man on fire.

3 It was such a spectacular explosion that one could not be unaware of it. The father's unwillingness to look, his clenched jaw, and his body hunched over the steering wheel all tell us he wanted only to get away from the scene of the accident. (Remainder of answer will vary.)

4 Individual answers will vary.

5 This question refers to the students' prediction of whether disaster would strike the poor mom-and-pop station or the rich franchise.

6 One reason for the father not stopping would be that he was afraid, not for himself, perhaps, but for his son and his son's friend. Another reason would be that the father did not know how he could help or thought that others were taking care of the situation. Students may point out that he was a doctor, the one person who might have been able to help in the disaster.

7 The explanation will certainly ring true to many readers. Younger idealistic readers may have trouble accepting that people often lack the courage, compassion, or knowledge to help others and, therefore, see this reasoning as rationalization. More mature readers will be more likely to agree with the author's analysis.

8 Problems often left to experts are the hole in the ozone, the destruction of the rain forest, and the proper disposal of nuclear waste. Whether students agree that we should leave these problems to the experts or try to participate in solutions ourselves will depend on several factors: how socially active they are, how educated they are, or how responsible or empowered they feel.

9 Individual answers will vary.

See *General Organization and Guidelines,* page viii, in the *Introduction* for comments on **PART 2**.

PART 3

FURTHER READING, WRITING, AND DISCUSSION

Ⓐ Preparing to read

REFLECTION AND DISCUSSION

Answers (page 151)

1 Dr. King felt he needed to clarify his position against the war because the war had gotten worse (intensified) and its effects on the United States more destructive. He was also upset by people saying that peace and civil rights didn't mix; in so saying, they showed they did not understand Dr. King's commitment to all who suffer and not just to his own people.

2 Dr. King did not feel the United States could solve Vietnam's problems because a solution would require the efforts of the two Vietnamese factions in the conflict. Further, he felt the war was filled with complexities and ambiguities that made it unlikely that either side was right or virtuous. Dr. King also hints at the immorality of war or violence as a solution to problems.

3 Readers can only surmise an answer. As a preacher, or man of religion, Dr. King's perspective on life and world events likely had a more moral base than the average person's. Students may see a connection between the suffering of the poor people Dr. King championed in the United States and the suffering of the Vietnamese people in the war. (Concrete answers will come as students read further.)

Ⓑ Reading for overall meaning

Answers (page 151)

We know that Dr. King was just as concerned about the Vietnamese victims of war as he was about U.S. victims when he tells us 1) that he could not segregate his moral concern; 2) that his Christian ministry obligated him to seek peace; and 3) that it was his belief that voiceless victims and even people we call enemies are our brothers. In a sense, all of these are contained in this statement: "Justice is indivisible."

Ⓔ Discussion: Critical thinking

Answers (page 153)

1 Students may interpret "Justice is indivisible" in different ways. In light of Dr. King's reasons for opposing the war, we take it to mean that justice cannot exist for some if it does not exist for all. It cannot exist for well-off people if it doesn't exist for poorer people, minorities, and even so-called enemies in another country.

2 Individual answers will vary. Students will probably be able to give examples of rules and laws that have little to do with morality or doing the right thing.

3 Individual answers will vary. This is a tough question. Students may need some time to think their way to an answer.

PART 4

FOCUS ON WRITING SKILLS

B Meeting reader expectations: Persuasive essays

EXERCISE 2 *Teacher persuasive essay*

Answers (page 157)

1 Individual answers will vary.

2 The thesis statement is the last sentence in the introduction: *To know that I can be both patriotic and against war, I need only think carefully about the definition of patriotism, consider what my religion tells me about war, and look at the economic and human losses that war has brought to the world.* (Remainder of answer will vary.)

3 There are three body paragraphs that support the thesis: the first on the definition of patriotism, the second on religious reasons for opposing war, and the third on losses incurred in wars. Opinions will vary regarding the most and least persuasive paragraphs.

4 We know from the title of Exercise 2 that the writer is a teacher. We learn that the writer has participated in antiwar demonstrations and supports conscientious objectors. We learn about his religious background, which opposes all war. It does not seem that the author has been a soldier; if he had been, he would likely have used something from that experience in his essay.

5 Individual answers will vary.

EXERCISE 3 *Correcting for consistency in tense*

Answers (page 157)

Our teacher let us out of class early so that we *could* go to a lecture on campus one day last week. The lecture began late, so we *had* to wait. I am usually impatient, so I *became* upset when we had to wait 15 minutes for the talk to begin. Since I know a lot about geology, I was able to follow the lecture, but many of my classmates *couldn't*. I noticed that one of my classmates, Mario, *was* sleeping. Fortunately, our teacher *wasn't* there because I think she would have been angry with him.

EXERCISE 4 *Correcting for consistency in person and number*

Sample answers (page 158)

1 Anyone can learn a foreign language if *he* or *she studies.*

2 Everyone has the ability to learn, so students should never give up when it seems difficult to *them.*

3 *One* also *needs* to keep in mind that *some (students)* might be better at oral skills than at reading and writing, and vice versa.

4 Students should be proud of their strengths but at the same time be willing to work on *their* weaknesses.

5 Students often focus on vocabulary, but *they* need to realize that vocabulary is only one part of a language.

6 *Language learners* should remember that they can't communicate without knowing the structure and phonology of a language.

EXERCISE 5 *Avoiding the informal* you

Sample answers (page 159)

1 During the afternoon, when it's very hot in my country, *a person needs* to dress in cooler clothes.

2 *One* should try to avoid wearing dark colors.

3 *Shorts can't be worn* in public in my country, however.

4 People consider wearing shorts indecent, so shorts aren't suitable for *a person* to wear.

5 At home, of course, *a person* can wear whatever *he or she wants.*

6 If *company arrives,* though, *an effort should be made* to look presentable.

EXERCISE 6 *Correcting for consistency in tone*

Answers (page 160)

1 John *didn't attend* his math class to prepare for his history exam.

2 It was difficult to give the accident victim the necessary medical attention because he was *shrieking with pain.*

3 Two *men* approached the managing editor's office to see what the excitement was about.

4 A family with many *children* will find making ends meet more difficult.

5 Marcella remarked that John's new sunglasses were *very fashionable.*

6 Smaller children often refuse to eat vegetables, which they find *unappetizing.*

7 Archie will probably have trouble selling his car for a good price because it is *old and in bad condition.*

8 The students reported that they had had a *very enjoyable* time on their spring vacation.

EXERCISE 7 *Editing for consistency in tense, person, number, and tone*

Sample answers (page 161)

The issue of doing what is right can be a difficult one for a foreign student. Sometimes the difference in how two cultures viewed things was extreme. It can even drive you nuts. I remember once my instructor asked to see me in her office later that afternoon. I agreed to see her at 3:00, but then my sister calls me on my cell phone from her car. She says she has a flat tire and is waiting on the side of the highway. Of course, I went to help her out. In the next class with the professor, she was very aggressive and asked why I don't keep my appointment. I guess I should have called her, but in the urgency of my sister's call, I forget to. My professor was real mad. To this day, she treats me like a liar–she doubted every word I say now. How are you supposed to act in a culture where a silly appointment is more important than my family?

The issue of doing what is right can be a difficult one for a foreign student. Sometimes the difference in how two cultures *view* things *is* extreme. It can even drive a *person to distraction.* I remember once my instructor asked to see me in her office later that afternoon. I agreed to see her at 3:00, but then my sister *called* me on my cell phone from her car. She *said* she *had* a flat tire and *was* waiting on the side of the highway. Of course, I went to help her out. In the next class with the professor, she was very aggressive and asked why I *hadn't kept* my appointment. I *suppose* I should have called her, but in the urgency of my sister's call, I *forgot* to. My professor was *really angry.* To this day, she treats me like a liar–she *doubts* every word I say now. How *is a person* supposed to act in a culture where a silly appointment is more important than *one's* family?

PART 5

FORMAL WRITING ASSIGNMENT

See *General Organization and Guidelines,* page xi, in the *Introduction* for additional comments on this part.

Ⓐ Writing topics (page 162)

As mentioned in *General Comments* on page 39, you should encourage students to come up with other propositions dealing with the topic if the ones given are not attractive to them. If there are too many topics from which to choose, however, the choice can be more difficult rather than easier, so you may want to limit students to three topics. Also, if you decide to do panel discussions to generate ideas, it will be very time-consuming if there are more than two or three topics, as each topic will require its own panel.

CHAPTER 7

Progress and Tradition

....

For the discussion in Part 1 – and the rest of the lesson – to make sense, students will have to make a distinction between *standard of living* and *quality of life. Standard of living* is the level of subsistence and comfort in everyday life enjoyed by a country. It is a pretty objective measure of what goods, services, and infrastructure a country has. *Quality of life,* on the other hand, is more subjective, so it will have different meanings for different people. A country with a low standard of living could be judged to have a high quality of life if it met subjective criteria like warm personal relations among people, low crime rates, and a comfortable pace of life, for example. Obviously, there is overlap between the two terms, but they should not be used interchangeably by students.

The core writing assignment in this lesson is an argument paper. An argument paper differs slightly from a traditional essay in organization and content. In an argument paper, students present their side of an argument, the other side, and then bring the two together to show why they prefer the side they have chosen. In a standard essay or even a persuasive paper, writers would not normally deal with the antithesis, i.e., the other side. In an argument paper, they do.

Teachers can look at the assignment as a way to improve students' thinking and writing in general. In considering the opposite view, students are forced to think more carefully about their own view. Therefore, an argument paper is not so much an end in itself as a useful exercise to improve essay writing in general.

Part 4, *Sentence Grammar,* deals with parallelism.

....

INTRODUCTION TO THE TOPIC, READING, AND DISCUSSION

C Preparing to read

PREVIEWING THE VOCABULARY

Answers (page 167)

1 c	**4** c	**7** a	**10** c
2 c	**5** b	**8** c	
3 a	**6** b	**9** b	

D Reading for overall meaning

Answers (page 168)

Urbanization and advances in technology have given people more material things like nice houses and cars but have made them too independent, lonelier, more depressed, and like parts in a machine.

E Reading for more detail

Answers (page 172)

1 He does not heal them, for he has no healing powers. He does, however, try to help by sharing in their suffering.

2 The Dalai Lama tells us the basic question in everyone's life is, "How am I to be happy?" (Remainder of answer will vary.)

3 According to the Dalai Lama, people in rich countries have the outside trappings of wealth but are poor on the inside: they are less satisfied and less happy than poorer people and suffer more from emotional problems like anxiety, discontent, frustration, uncertainty, and depression. People in poor countries, who may suffer from more physical ailments, have a richer emotional life: they feel more satisfied and more a part of their community because of their dependence on others.

4 Initially, he finds everything very pleasant and everyone very friendly. As time passes, he begins to see isolation and depression beneath the surface, and he senses the troubled atmosphere created by people's problems and concerns.

5 Modern life is characterized by materialism, with people scurrying around seeking to obtain more and more, according to the Dalai Lama. It is an urban life which leads people to rely on machines and services rather than other people. It also leads to greater autonomy, or independence from others. People see their lives as dependent on their jobs or bosses rather than on their neighbors, with a resulting lack of caring about neighbors.

6 Individual answers will vary.

See *General Organization and Guidelines,* page viii, in the *Introduction* for comments on **PART 2**.

PART 3

FURTHER READING, WRITING, AND DISCUSSION

Ⓐ Preparing to read

REFLECTION AND DISCUSSION (page 175)

This section is necessarily long to prepare students for the tough vocabulary and some of the new ideas in the reading. However, the time spent here will save students time later when they read; the discussion should also create interest in the reading itself.

Ⓑ Reading for overall meaning

Answers (page 175)

Pitroda sees a connection between the technical and social benefits, but we get the feeling the social benefits are more important to him.

Ⓔ Discussion: Critical thinking

Answers (page 178)

1 Students will probably have different answers. Certainly, a case can be made that his thinking and writing reflect both his Indian background *and* his U.S. experience. His background shows in the compassion and insight with which he describes conditions in his home country. Some may see his dynamic approach to problem solving as a U.S. characteristic; certainly we would expect his U.S. graduate studies to have affected his thinking as well.

2 The Dalai Lama does not appear to be concerned with social change in the same sense that Pitroda is interested in helping the poor improve their standard of living. While the Dalai Lama sees the evils of technology, Pitroda sees the advantages of social leveling that comes from technology.

3 Individual answers will vary. Their caring is similar in that both men are sincere about the people whose problems they deal with. It is different in that the Dalai Lama seems primarily interested in helping people in rich countries. Pitroda, on the other hand, focuses on people who are poor. Looked at another way, the Dalai Lama focuses on problems of a spiritual or emotional nature while Pitroda focuses on problems in the physical sphere.

4 Individual answers will vary.

PART 4

FOCUS ON WRITING SKILLS

B Meeting reader expectations: Avoiding logical fallacies

EXERCISE 2 *Recognizing logical fallacies*

Part B: Logical fallacies

Answers (page 180)

1 c	**4** d
2 e	**5** f
3 a	**6** b

EXERCISE 3 *Fixing logical fallacies*

Sample answers (page 180)

1 The increase in cancer in our community may be the result of the nuclear reactor recently built nearby.

2 Although some critics point out shortcomings in Canada's health care system, most Canadian and many U.S. experts find it successful.

3 A vote for Ms. X is a vote for a more conservative governor who will cut taxes and important services in our state.

4 Many scientists believe that global warming will destroy our planet.

EXERCISE 4 *Identifying and correcting logical fallacies*

Answers (page 181)

_X_ **1** The statement begs the question. Many developing countries are industrializing in an effort to develop their economies, but industrialization is not the only means to the end. Many other countries have developed through their vast oil reserves, and Pitroda has shown us that a technological innovation can help a country develop.

_X_ **2** This is an emotional appeal. It implies that if we want to be sensible, we have to agree with the writer. The fallacy ignores many means of development that do not pollute.

_X_ **3** This argument fails because it is circular: it merely repeats itself. Countries all over the world are modernizing, some with aid and some without.

_X_ **4** By begging the question, this statement ignores the tendency for economic problems to become political ones. Evidence is provided by political campaigns in Mexico, the United States, and other places where the state of the economy has played a major role.

_X_ **5** This circular argument is at the same time an emotional appeal playing on people's skepticism of politicians. Some, many, or most politicians may be corrupt; all of them could not be.

_X_ **6** Again, a circular argument sounds convincing because it supports itself. However, one cannot intelligently maintain that developed countries are responsible for all the world's ills when evidence to the contrary exists.

_X_ **7** This sweeping generalization ignores, among other views, the view of many experts that financial aid is the key to development.

EXERCISE 5 *Student model of an argument essay*

Answers (first reading) (page 181)

1 Individual answers will vary.

2 Individual answers will vary, but he does appear to avoid logical fallacies.

Answers (second reading) (page 183)

1 Mr. Orozco's thesis appears in the last sentence of the introduction: *It is a mistake to look only at the material side and to ignore the spiritual side when considering quality of life.*

2 He discusses spiritual matters in paragraph 2. He discusses material matters in paragraph 3.

3 In paragraph 4, he makes it clear that spiritual matters are more important than material ones.

4 Individual answers will vary.

5 He makes a connection between quality of life, in his opinion dominated by spiritual matters, and social welfare. (Remainder of answer will vary.)

6 Paragraph 4 shows his voice most strongly because he uses real examples from his life. His voice is evident in the whole essay, as well. The reader feels Mr. Orozco is expressing his own point of view, realizing it may not be a popular one for his audience.

EXERCISE 6 *Making segments parallel*

Sample answers (page 184)

1 India is the seventh largest country in the world in area but second in *population*.

2 India's population is distributed unevenly, with four-fifths living in villages and the rest *living* in towns and cities.

3 India's climate varies from tropical heat in the South to *near-Arctic cold in the North Rajasthan Desert.*

4 Geographical features include the highest mountains in the world, the Himalayas, and *some of the most densely populated regions of the world, the Ganges Plain.*

5 India's cultural heritage, including architecture, dance, literature, music, philosophy, and sculpture, is one of the richest *and most ancient in the world.*

EXERCISE 7 *More practice in making segments parallel*

Sample answers (page 184)

1 The workforce numbers 286 million people, but this figure does not include the unemployed *or secondary workers.*

2 Secondary workers, who do not receive their main support from their work activities, include people involved in household industry *or in cultivation.*

3 According to a recent census, more than 67 percent of the workforce was employed in agriculture, 15 percent *in manufacturing,* and 18 percent in services.

4 In recent decades India has experienced a "brain drain" of educated and trained Indians to other countries because of unemployment and *underemployment.*

5 Many educated Indians prefer to seek jobs abroad or *to work* in foreign companies located in India.

EXERCISE 8 *Editing for parallelism*

Sample answers (page 185)

   In his discussion of developing countries, Schumacher says that dual economies create political problems *and social tensions.* Every country has poor people *as well as rich people.* However, in a dual economy, the difference between the two groups is so great that a cultural gap develops between the two groups. The rich, a small percentage, typically live in the capital or *the second largest city.* The poor live in the country or *in towns.* The problem is that most development efforts go to the big cities and help the rich. The gap between the poor and *the rich* increases as the rich benefit from the changes and the poor do not.

PART 5

FORMAL WRITING ASSIGNMENT

See *General Organization and Guidelines,* page xi, in the *Introduction* for additional comments on this part.

Ⓑ Generating ideas: A debate (page 186)

A debate is a time-consuming, challenging activity. However, since the topic of the chapter is a difficult one to think about and to write on, students may need this extra activity to help formulate their position on the topic. You may have a sense that students are ready to write without a debate; it may still be helpful to them to have small group discussions on the topic where they brainstorm and discuss rather than debate.

MORE ON GRAMMAR AND PUNCTUATION

....

1 SENTENCE STRUCTURE

Ⓐ General sentence structure

EXERCISE 1 *Identifying sentence structure*

Answers (page 191)

1 Correct: a, b, d, f

  Incorrect: Item c uses a preposition (in spite of) as if it were a conjunction.
  Item e needs either *although* or *but*, not both.

2 Correct: a, b, d, e

  Incorrect: Item c uses the preposition *because of* as if it were a conjunction.

3 Correct: a, b, c

  Incorrect: Item d would be correct if it the punctuation were changed: *It was a difficult book; however, Allie finished it.*

4 Correct: a, c, d, e

  Incorrect: Item b has good sentence structure, but the meaning is wrong.

Ⓑ Transition words

EXERCISE 2 *Identifying correct structure and punctuation*

Answers (page 193)

1 Correct: b, d

  Incorrect: Even if item a were written as one sentence, the meaning would be wrong.
  The punctuation in item c creates a comma splice.

2 Correct: a, c, d

  Incorrect: The punctuation in item b creates a comma splice.

3 Correct: b, c, d, e

  Incorrect: Item d, correctly formed, shows why item a is wrong.

2 RELATIVE CLAUSES

EXERCISE 3 *Recognizing good relative clauses*

Answers (page 196)

__✓__ **1** The city water department needs a secretary who can do word processing.

__X__ **2** A penalty will be added to bills which is paid late. → A penalty will be added to bills *which are paid late*.

__X__ **3** I bought some notebooks on sale which they are not of very good quality. → I bought some notebooks on sale *which are not of very good quality.*

__✓__ **4** When is that library book we used for our report due?

__✓__ **5** Professor Chavez, who you know as the author of our economics text, will deliver a guest lecture next Friday.

__X__ **6** He is a good speaker who his accomplishments are known to all. → He is a good speaker *whose accomplishments are known to all.*

__X__ **7** Can you recommend a restaurant who serves fish? → Can you recommend a restaurant *that serves fish?*

__✓__ **8** Can you recommend a restaurant where fish is served?

__X__ **9** Firefighters whose work can be very dangerous are often paid less than police officers or aren't paid at all. → Firefighters, *whose work can be very dangerous,* are often paid less than police officers or aren't paid at all.

__X__ **10** I'm afraid that the cassette I am listening to it is defective. Can I get another copy? → I'm afraid that the cassette *I am listening to* is defective.

__X__ **11** It is sometimes difficult to convince students who their only goal is to pass the TOEFL that ability is more important than test results. → It is sometimes difficult to convince students *whose only goal is to pass the TOEFL* that ability is more important than test results.

__✓__ **12** Is that the company you wrote your letter of complaint to?

__✓__ **13** I removed an egg from a carton that was damaged.

EXERCISE 4 *Adding relative clauses to sentences*

Answers (page 196)

1 Professor Norris, *who used to direct the English language program,* is an excellent administrator. (a)

2 Computers, *which have come down in price,* are becoming more widespread worldwide. (a)

3 The police haven't been able to locate the witness, *whose testimony is important to the case.* (b)

4 I would like a car *that doesn't require a lot of maintenance.* (b)

5 The book bag *I bought* isn't big enough for all the books I need this semester. (a)

6 People *who live in glass houses* shouldn't throw stones. (a)

7 Students *who read a lot* usually find that their writing improves. (b)

8 Punctuation, *which often frustrates writing students,* is not terribly difficult to learn to use correctly. (a)

9 I gave him the letter *he asked for.* (a)

10 My sister-in-law, *who I introduced you to once,* is coming to visit soon. (a)

11 We bought two kilograms of rice, *most of which we'll prepare for the party.* (b)

12 We've invited a lot of people, *most of whom you know,* to the party. (b)

13 They want to go someplace *where they can be alone.* (b)

14 Pam gave me a lot of advice, *most of which wasn't useful.* (b)

···················

3 WORD ORDER

Ⓐ Adverbials

EXERCISE 5 *Using adverbials*

Answers (page 199)

Manner: punctually, without looking, carelessly, in a hurry, meaningfully

Place: to the store, at home, here, on campus

Time: since Monday, late, early, on my birthday, recently

EXERCISE 6 *Correct word order*

Answers (page 199)

1 He doesn't always brush his teeth after meals.

2 I seldom have time to cook lunch at home on weekdays.

3 It rarely snows in my country in the winter.

4 They usually celebrate his birthday with a big party in a restaurant at night.

5 Do you ever go to the movies with friends on the weekend?

6 I have never been able to understand the reason for his strange behavior.

7 Is George likely to leave his homework at home again?

8 I don't usually have trouble doing my homework without interruptions in a quiet place.

9 There aren't too many people in line at the post office right now.

10 She has never wanted to go out with them on the weekend.

11 Seldom do I have time to read stories a second time.

12 I had never experienced such rude behavior.
Never had I experienced such rude behavior.

EXERCISE 7 *Adding modifiers to sentences*

Answers (page 200)

1 I *almost* dropped my book on the floor.

2 Children *that are dependent* need their parents.

3 It took most of the students *nearly* three hours to write their compositions.

4 Some of them spent *only* 30 minutes doing it.

5 The students did not appreciate another assignment *that was so difficult* from their teacher.

6 This task is so simple that *even* a three-year-old can do it.

7 *Without looking at them,* the teacher asked a question of the students, who answered quickly.

8 The cosmetic salesperson sprayed perfume samples *that smelled wonderful* on the customer.

9 Mary's unhealthy because she eats *hardly* anything. (Many native speakers would prefer and use this version, which is not better grammatically: Mary's unhealthy because she *hardly* eats anything.)

10 *Only* a mother knows what her children are really like.

EXERCISE 8 *Adding* also *and* too

Answers (page 201)

1 Tony took his parents sightseeing last weekend. He took them to his favorite restaurant, *too.*

2 His parents liked the places they visited. They *also* liked the food at the restaurant.

3 His parents usually visit Tony in May. This year they are *also* coming in September.

4 The Johnsons stay at a hotel when they visit Tony because he has a small apartment, and he has a roommate, *too.*

5 Tony is looking forward to their next visit. His aunt and uncle are going to visit, *too.*

6 His parents usually drive when they visit. His aunt and uncle *will also drive,* but in their own car.

7 Tony likes his uncle a lot. He *also* likes his aunt, but not as much.

EXERCISE 9 *Adding indirect objects to sentences*

Answers (page 202)

1 My parents didn't give *me* what I wanted for my birthday.

2 I had asked for a particular motorcycle, but they didn't buy it *for me.*

3 I was disappointed because I had told *them* which model I wanted.

4 Fortunately, several friends remembered to send *me* cards.

5 My mother also made a cake *for me*, so I was somewhat consoled about the motorcycle.

6 My parents also bought *me* a very nice sweater.

7 A friend has really admired the sweater, but I don't think I'll ever lend it *to him.*

8 I was telling *him* the truth when I said he could borrow anything else I had.

9 After I explained the situation *to him*, he was completely understanding.

10 I'm working part-time so that I can buy the motorcycle *for myself.*

11 I really don't expect my parents to give it *to me.*

12 I'll never say anything about the motorcycle *to them* again.

EXERCISE 10 *Completing sentences with direct and indirect objects*

Answers (page 203)

(Individual completions will vary.)

1 Mary gave John some flowers. She gave them to him reluctantly because (she didn't know if he would like them).

2 I'm going to send my brother a birthday card. I'll send it to him even though (he didn't send me one).

3 I don't understand this equation. Could you explain it to me so that (it makes sense)?

4 She told me a funny story. She had to tell it to me in a soft voice because (it might offend someone).

5 I hope you take better care of my notes this time. If you don't, I won't lend them to you (next time).

6 That is a very pretty sweater. Who made it for you?

7 I'm going to get my parents a TV for their anniversary. I'll try to buy <u>it for them</u> early so that (I can get a good deal).

8 My books are in your car. Could you bring <u>them to me</u> before you (go)?

9 I don't especially like that restaurant. I really can't recommend <u>it to you</u>.

····································

4 ADJECTIVES AND ADVERBS

Note: Many native speakers use adjectives in place of adverbs. This usage is either careless or is a sign of a change in North American English. Students may ask about signs they have seen like "Drive slow," which most English teachers would change to "Drive slowly."

Ⓐ Adjectives and adverbs with the same form

EXERCISE 11 *Using adjectives and adverbs*

Answers (page 205)

1 If you try *hard*, you will *surely* succeed.

2 The quiz was so *easy* that I finished very *quickly*.

3 I'm not very *good* at tennis, but I swim quite *well*.

4 You look very *handsome* today.

5 Let's finish this assignment *fast* so that we can go out.

6 He says he's got a cold, but he seems *well* to me.

7 I can't treat you to lunch because I *hardly* have enough money for myself.

8 The boss got *really* angry with the employees.

9 I will *gladly* lend him my car.

10 The new boss expects the employees to work more *efficiently* than they used to.

11 She isn't as *friendly* as her brother.

12 It's better to be *safe* than sorry.

EXERCISE 12 *Using comparative forms*

Answers (page 206)

1 You can do this *more easily* if you concentrate.

2 The *busier* he is, the more nervous he gets.

3 They moved to a *safer* neighborhood.

4 The class tends to get *noisier* when the teacher leaves the room.

5 He's trying to live *more healthily* by eating better.

6 I'm afraid I have to ask you to work a little *more quickly.*

7 Try to treat him a little *more nicely,* and I'm sure he'll cooperate.

8 He is much *slower* in reading than in math.

9 The composition was *easier* to do than I had expected.

10 They asked me to drive *more slowly.*

....

5 PUNCTUATION

Ⓐ Commas

EXERCISE 13 *Using commas for introductory and nonessential elements*

Answers (page 207)

1 On their vacation, the Slovins are going to go to India, which they've both been interested in visiting ever since an Indian family moved in next door.

2 Because of busy work schedules, they won't be able to spend more than two weeks there.

3 They'll visit the Taj Mahal, I'm sure, as well as two or three major cities.

4 Since the Slovins live in a warm climate, they already have suitable clothes for their trip.

5 They'll want to buy presents which are typical of the places that they visit.

6 In my opinion, they'll have a wonderful time because both are good travelers and interested in other cultures.

EXERCISE 14 *Using commas to separate independent clauses and items in a series*

Answers (page 208)

1 Jack, his brother, and I are going hiking and fishing this weekend.

2 We had wanted to go to the beach, but we couldn't get hotel accommodations.

3 We decided to go to the mountains instead and enjoy the cooler weather.

4 We'll probably hike for a few days, and then we'll relax by fishing at the local lake.

5 We'll take food, sleeping bags, a few changes of clothes, but little else.

6 Would you like to come along, or are you busy this weekend?

EXERCISE 15 *Using commas in addresses and dates*

Answers (page 208)

Individual answers will vary.

B Periods, semicolons, and colons

EXERCISE 16 *Using periods, semicolons, and colons*

Note: Items with semicolons (2, 6) could also be punctuated with periods. Likewise, items with periods (4, 7) could be punctuated with semicolons.

Answers (page 209)

1 Students who wish to improve their writing can do so in three ways: reading more, studying English rhetoric and sentence structure, and heeding their writing teacher's comments.

2 Punctuation is not very interesting to study; correct punctuation does, however, make writing easier to read.

3 The semicolon and the colon look similar and, therefore, are sometimes used incorrectly by students.

4 The period and the semicolon are almost identical in function. Each signals that an independent clause lies before and after it.

5 There is an important difference between the period and the semicolon: The semicolon is used within one longer sentence, while the period breaks up two independent clauses into separate sentences.

6 Students should be careful to use the right transition word; it is better to omit a transition word than to use it incorrectly.

7 By far the most mistakes are made with commas. They are often used unnecessarily.

8 An understanding of the basic rules of punctuation and a little practice are sufficient for most students to master punctuation, however.

EXERCISE 17 *Comparing expressions*

Answers (page 211)

1 Joan and Mike's car / Joan's and Mike's cars

In the first, Joan and Mike have one car together. / In the second, each one has one or more cars.

2 the boy's toys / the boys' toys

In the first, one boy has toys. / In the second, two or more boys have toys.

3 the waitress's uniforms / the waitresses' uniforms

One waitress has uniforms. / Waitresses have uniforms.

4 the lady's room / the ladies' room

a room which belongs to a lady / a room (often bathroom) for ladies

5 the wings of the airplane / the bird's wings

An *of*-phrase is typically used to denote possession with inanimate nouns (airplane). Animate nouns (bird) usually take -*'s*. Because of the typical -*'s* pattern for animate possession, English allows phrases like *the boy whose mother died's father.* Most people, however, would find an *of*-phrase a little more elegant in this situation: *the father of the boy whose mother died.*

6 my brother-in-law's work / my brother-in-law's working

The first is a possessive, work that my brother-in-law does. The second is a contraction for *brother-in-law is* and is not a possessive at all.

EXERCISE 18 *Adding apostrophes*

Answers (page 211)

1 Peg and Sue's Diner doesn't open until eight o'clock in the morning.

2 The students' assignments in Professor Brown's section are longer than ours.

3 My roommates' class schedules are easier than mine.

4 This year's winter lettuce crop was ruined by heavy rains.

5 Whose dress is Helen going to wear, yours or hers?

6 Who's going to meet Phyllis' flight tomorrow night—her husband or her sons?

7 Flight attendants' working hours are just as long as pilots'.

Ⓓ Quotation marks and indirect speech

EXERCISE 19 *Adding quotation marks*

Answers (page 212)

1 He asked me where I had been living.

2 I told him, "I have the same apartment that I had when I met you."

3 "Are you eating well," my mother always asks when she calls, "and do you have nice friends?"

4 I assure her that I can take care of myself and that she shouldn't worry.

5 The police wanted to know what we had seen during the accident.

6 We said, "We weren't really paying attention, so we don't know which driver was at fault."

7 "A stitch in time saves nine," our history professor is fond of telling us.

EXERCISE 20 *Editing for punctuation*

Answers (page 213)

In the essay "Whether, How, and Why to Spank," author David Dempsey presents his case in favor of physical punishment of children. David Dempsey explains, "Better to punish children than to be indifferent to them, since it is the neglected child who is more likely to grow up to be a problem." On the other hand, in his book <u>Dr. Spock on Parenting</u>, a respected doctor comes out against physical punishment. "If we are ever to turn toward a kinder society and a safer world," Dr. Spock writes, "a revulsion against the physical punishment of children would be a good place to start." "Whose advice should we follow?" parents raising children often ask. The answer to the question is not easy.